A Pattern for Family Living

God's Masterpiece

Relationships Within the Family

A Pattern for Family Living

God's Masterpiece

Relationships Within the Family

R.D. Henton

© Copyright 1995 — R.D. Henton

All rights reserved. This book is protected under the copyright laws of the United States of America. This book may not be copied or reprinted for commercial gain or profit. The use of short quotations or occasional page copying for personal or group study is permitted and encouraged. Permission will be granted upon request. Unless otherwise identified, Scripture quotations are from the King James Version of the Bible.

Take note that the name satan and related names are not capitalized. We choose not to acknowledge him, even to the point of violating grammatical rules.

Treasure House
An Imprint of
Destiny Image, Inc.®
P.O. Box 310
Shippensburg, PA 17257-0310

"For where your treasure is
there will your heart be also." Matthew 6:21

ISBN 1-56043-775-8

For Worldwide Distribution
Printed in the U.S.A.

Treasure House books are available through these fine distributors outside the United States:

Christian Growth, Inc.
Jalan Kilang-Timor, Singapore 0315

Rhema Ministries Trading
Randburg, South Africa

Salvation Book Centre
Petaling, Jaya, Malaysia

Successful Christian Living
Capetown, Rep. of South Africa

Vine Christian Centre
Mid Glamorgan, Wales, United Kingdom

Vision Resources
Ponsonby, Auckland, New Zealand

WA Buchanan Company
Geebung, Queensland, Australia

Word Alive
Niverville, Manitoba, Canada

Inside the U.S., call toll free to order:
1-800-722-6774

Contents

	Introduction	vii
Chapter 1	Mankind: God's Masterpiece	1
Chapter 2	Man: God's Crown	17
Chapter 3	Woman: Helpmeet and More	31
Chapter 4	The Virtuous Woman	45
Chapter 5	Marriage in the Will of God	61
Chapter 6	Making Marriage Work	73
Chapter 7	Likewise You Husbands	89
Chapter 8	God Has Even More in Store for You	105

Chapter 9   Household Salvation 119
Chapter 10 There Is Hope for Broken Homes ... 133
Chapter 11 Final Things 147

Introduction

Marriage, as it regards family and the home, is an important, timely, and controversial subject. As a pastor and father, I have dealt with the temptations, the trials, the failures, and the successes of every type and degree in the lives of men, women, and children. In every case, I have become more and more convinced that the making of man by God was a masterpiece work. As a physical being, man stands tall—with 206 bones, 633 muscles, and a brain capable of storing more than five times the data contained in the greatest library in the world: the Library of Congress. Man, using his ingenuity, constructs the best houses, the tallest buildings, and the longest bridges. Still, with all their talents and abilities, men and women often fall short as husbands and wives, fathers and mothers.

Man was created to be one with his Master, but he chose sin instead. Through sin, he fell out of fellowship with God and brought upon himself the numerous problems he faces today. One of the problems he faces today, as a consequence of sin, is the destruction of many marriages. Man was made to lead and guide family and home. But by giving in to satanic power, man precipitated marital disruption, confusion, discontent, violence, and even death.

In this book I deal with the role of the New Testament wife, and I accentuate the virtues of a wife and mother in today's world. As a mother, the wife nurtures the children, manages the household, saves for the future, and often contributes to the family income. I also address the responsibilities of the man as husband and father, as the head of the home, and as an example for the children. Through this book, I am sounding a gong and calling for level-headed thinking as I offer help to wives and husbands alike so that they can stay on track.

We must begin by understanding the role of the individual partners in marriage, as well as by accepting the fact that marriage is in the will of God. Marriage is a sacred institution that emanated from the Eternal, who continues to sanction it today in Holy Writ. This book also points out the importance of men and women exercising care in selecting their respective mates. A responsible choice sets the stage to fulfill God's will for marriage. Caution, consideration, and communication must be used and combined to preserve the sanctity of the marriage and to maintain a secure and tranquil home.

For this to be accomplished, it is necessary for couples to understand the importance of priorities. Marriage based on the biblical model begins with the proper structure: the head of every woman is man; the head of every man is Christ; and the head of Christ is God. Secular society, together with many religious groups, has abandoned this model and substituted another rather than embrace the Creator's plan—a fact that accounts for the unholy condition of marriage and families in the world today. I see parents who are in direct opposition to one another and children who oppose one or both parents. Families are ripped apart by dissension and animosity. As children grow up, they encounter personal problems with nowhere to turn for support, thereby stifling their normal, wholesome development as children. Children need a wise and caring father and mother to turn to for counsel and direction.

The beginning of the solution to this problem is in turning to the saving grace of Jesus Christ: He is the only One capable of bringing and preserving peace, understanding, and patience. He is the only One who can establish a home based on love and commitment. Through Him, those who are willing to follow His example will find ample power to deal with the problems they face. With the overcoming presence of Jesus Christ in their hearts and lives, each man and each woman will emerge as the husband, wife, father, and mother God intends them to be. The Savior, Jesus Christ, remains the radiant Star of Hope for all disturbed marriages, broken homes, wayward children, and inconsiderate and irresponsible parents. He is the one and only Panacea for all who will turn to and rely on Him for their salvation.

As you read this book, open your heart and your mind. I know the Spirit of God will work in you and through you, if you are willing to become all He intends you to be.

Chapter 1

Mankind: God's Masterpiece

And God said, Let Us make man in Our image, after Our likeness: and let them have dominion over the fish of the sea, and over the fowl of the air, and over the cattle, and over all the earth, and over every creeping thing that creepeth upon the earth. So God created man in His own image, in the image of God created He him; male and female created He them. And God blessed them, and God said unto them, Be fruitful, and multiply, and replenish the earth, and subdue it: and have dominion over the fish of the sea, and over the fowl of the air, and over every living thing that moveth upon the earth.

Genesis 1:26-28

As you read these words describing God's final act of creation, I want you to contemplate the wonder of this final act. Man was God's crowning achievement, His masterpiece among His creation. Of all that God had accomplished in the time prior to the creation of man, God declared it "good," but when He looked upon the creation of man, that part of His creation who was in His own image, the Word says, "behold, it was very good" (Gen. 1:31). You should take time right now and say these words: "I am God's masterpiece."

It is important for us to understand that we are not something created from the leftovers of creation. God didn't look around and say, "Oh, there is still some stuff left. I think I will make something from the leftovers." No, we are not made from the leftovers. Rather, we were reserved to the very end so that all creation would know we were the crowning achievement of God's work. It is true: God did save the very best for last. If we would realize who we are, we would not allow ourselves to become less than God wants us to be. Here is what the psalmist had to say about man:

> **When I consider Thy heavens, the work of Thy fingers, the moon and the stars, which Thou hast ordained; what is man, that Thou art mindful of him? and the son of man, that Thou visitest him? For Thou hast made him a little lower than the angels, and hast crowned him with glory and honour. Thou madest him to have dominion over the works of Thy hands: Thou hast put all things under his feet.**
>
> **Psalm 8:3-6**

The Age of Lucifer and His Fall

Before we can fully appreciate God's decision to create man and His ultimate plan for man, we need to know something about the process of creation. In the first verse in the Book of Genesis, we have the phrase, "In the beginning...." The Holy Bible continues from this point and records the history of creation from this time forward. The story of the creation of man is the beginning of the Antediluvian Age, or the age beginning with the end of the six days of creation and continuing to the flood of Noah. There are many, many thousands of years before the creation of man. Only God knows the time of the beginning, but, basically, the record we have is from 6,000 years ago to the present.

God told Adam and Eve to be fruitful and multiply and replenish the earth. Notice the word *replenish*. He also told Noah to be fruitful and multiply and replenish the earth, but we would expect to see this with Noah. All of life outside the ark had been destroyed in the flood, so Noah would naturally replenish what was destroyed. The fact that God told Adam to replenish the earth tells us that something existed before this record of creation.

The thousands of years of creation, prior to man's creation and the Antediluvian Age, is referred to as the Antechaotic Age. This is the age in which the angels ruled the earth with Lucifer as the chief angel. Although we don't have the full story concerning the events that took place between verses 1 and 2 of chapter 1 of the Book of Genesis, we do know something about Lucifer and the angels. Isaiah 14:12-15 tells us of Lucifer's fall, which brought chaos and destruction to the earth. More is said about Lucifer than about all the angelic hosts put together. Lucifer is actually a beautiful name. It means "son of the morning" and refers to the day star or the morning star, the brightest star in the sky, the son of dawn. According to the Book of Ezekiel, Lucifer was sound in wisdom and perfect in beauty. He walked up and down on stones of fire and had glittering stones all over his body. Every precious stone imaginable sparkled from his body, and he was in charge of the Eden of God. (See Ezekiel 28:12-14.) This was the status of Lucifer in the Antechaotic Age, before the 6,000-year period that begins in Genesis 1:26.

When God said the earth was without form and void, there was darkness on the face of the deep. The earth was without form and void as a result of Lucifer's attempt to ascend into the heavens. Apparently he wasn't in the heavens, but in the Eden of God. Because of Lucifer's attempt to set up his own throne and kingdom in the heavens, God took his authority from him and cast him down into hell. The Scriptures tell us there was a war. I don't know how long the war lasted or the details of the war, but I know that a third of the stars, or angels, were cast out of Heaven with Lucifer (see Rev. 12).

Whatever beauty Lucifer and the angels had before their fall, it was taken from them when God cast them down. When Lucifer and the angels hit the earth, volcanos erupted, mountains turned inside out, and hills turned upside down. The earth was in complete chaos. God took a mantle of darkness and covered the whole earth, and the earth had no shape or form. I do not know how long this condition lasted, but the time came when God decided to put His creation back in order again. Meanwhile, Lucifer had been stripped of his sovereignty, and he no longer ruled or had dominion over the earth. God transformed him into a devil monster, satan, and the angels who fell with him were transformed into demons. There was nothing pretty about the devil or his demons. That's why he comes as an angel of light or as a wolf wrapped up in sheep's clothing. When he entered the serpent, he brought a curse on the serpent. Prior to satan's entering it, the serpent walked upright and was a beautiful creature. Because of satan, God cursed the serpent and said, "Upon thy belly shalt thou go, and dust shalt thou eat all the days of thy life" (Gen. 3:14b).

Man Is Created in God's Image

When God created man, He made him an upright creature. God could have put a long tail behind us. God could have put fur down our back. God could have put feathers all over our bodies, but He chose to make us in His image and after His own likeness. Because we are like God, we don't have to eat off the ground like a wild animal. God gave us intelligence; He clothed us with glory and honor. Not only did He clothe us, but He also crowned us. We are the crowning masterpiece of God's creation.

Man became a living soul when God took the dust of the ground, formed his body, and blew into his nostrils the breath of life. Although we don't have God's nose or chin or eyes, we are in His image as a triune being. He is Father, Son, and Holy Ghost, and we are body, soul, and spirit. In the Book of First Thessalonians Paul prays that our "whole spirit and soul and body be preserved blameless unto the coming of our Lord Jesus Christ" (1 Thess. 5:23).

Don't allow God's masterpiece in you to be in vain. For some reason, man wants to act or be like everything except what God made him to be and do. For the past 6,000 years, man has defied God. There was a time when, according to Genesis 6:6, God repented of His decision to create man. God was grieved because man decided to go his own way rather than walk upright in the image of the Creator. Although God made man a little lower than the angels, He made him above the animals. Why have we resorted to animal names for so many of our dances today? We ought to reach up and try to find a dance acceptable to the angels. We might try a dance called the cherubim instead of the dance we call the "Dog" or the "Monkey" or the "Camel Walk." The world also had dances called the "Eagle Rock," the "Gorilla," and the "Snake." Why do we want to rate ourselves so low, when God made us above all that? The situation is just like the movie *Frankenstein*. This monster's master created it from pieces taken from everywhere. In the end the monster turns on its master. This is what the enemy has done to man.

Lucifer said, "I will be as the Most High. I will be as God." When he deceived Eve, he told her, "Ye shall not surely die...your eyes shall be opened, and ye shall be as gods..." (Gen. 3:4-5). Since the devil couldn't be as God, he lied to Eve and convinced her that she could be as God by eating of the tree of the knowledge of good and evil. Satan is selling that same lie to folks today. He wants to convince you that the only god you need is you. Satan is behind the New Age message, which says that you are God.

I know you are not God and you know that you are not God. You will let me down every time, but the God I serve never lets me down. Next thing I know, you will try to convince me that I am a descendant of a monkey. Perhaps you have heard the saying, "Once I was a tadpole trying to be, then I was a frog with movement so free, then I became a monkey in a bamboo tree, but now I'm a professor with a Ph.D."

If a monkey could talk, he would be the first to tell you that you did not come from him. He would tell you, "There are several ways I know you didn't evolve from me. I don't use drugs or smoke pot. I don't hijack cars or do drive-by shootings. I don't desert my babies on doorsteps or leave them in alleys. I don't beat up or rob senior citizens. I don't gamble my money away. I don't have to attend Alcoholics Anonymous or Gamblers Anonymous because I don't have those problems. I don't curse, swear, or take the Lord's name in vain. You will never hear me say, 'There is no God' and you will never hear me say, 'I am God.'"

We have to realize that we are God's masterpiece. God didn't make us serpents crawling on our belly, even though some of us act like serpents. God didn't make us a dog, even though some of us have the spirit of a dog. What we need to realize is that when God made us, He made us the best of His creation. We are the top of the line. Don't you know we grieve God just like our children grieve us? Every parent wants his or her child to have what the parent didn't have. You probably said, "When I grow up, my child is not going to have the same broken toy that he had last Christmas." My mother would put my toys up, and I thought I had lost them. I was afraid to tell her that I left my truck outside and that somebody had stolen it. I was afraid to tell her, and I figured what she didn't know didn't hurt. But, during Christmas, she would reach up on the shelf and get that same little toy truck I thought I had lost. And do you know what? That broken toy was just as good to me as if it were brand-new because I missed it.

I said to myself, "If I ever have children, they're not going to work on last year's broken toy." So the Lord blessed me to keep that vow. God has an investment in us and has shown kindness toward us so as to bring out the best in us. Consider the dominion He gave us over the fish of the sea and over the fowls of the air. He gave Adam the privilege of naming all the creatures and told him to subdue the earth, be fruitful, multiply, and replenish the earth because man was the top of the line.

Be All God Intends for You to Be!

God took one of man's own ribs, and with it He made woman. As men, we should thank God that we are two-fisted, thoroughbred men. Women also should thank God that they are women in every way, yes, total women. They may not have the hat they would like to put on their head, and they may not have the clothes they think they ought to have. But each can say, "Thank God I'm a total woman." Men may not have an automobile to ride in, but each can thank God for having made him a total man.

The Bible reads that the head of every woman is the man; the head of every man is Christ; and the head of Christ is God (see 1 Cor. 11:3). So we have four in the parade. Suppose everyone in the parade was walking down the avenue of time to the drumbeat of Heaven. God is in front with Jesus at His right side. Man is behind Jesus, and the woman is behind the man. You hear the parade coming down the avenue of time, and everything is working fine. Then, all of a sudden, something gets into the man, and he decides that he doesn't want to be a man anymore. He decides he wants to be a he-woman. Then something gets in the woman, and she decides that she doesn't want to be a woman anymore. She decides she wants to be a she-man. When God and Jesus look behind them, half the parade is gone because what God made in the beginning decided to change.

What disgusts me is the silence of church leaders about sexual life styles. They don't want to address issues that might cause a stir. I'm here to tell you that God will deliver men and women from the sin of homosexuality. It is not a civil rights issue. It is a moral issue. I know a Man who can set you free and put you on the street called "Straight." I'm here to tell you God is able to make all grace abound toward those who will look to

Him for deliverance. God can pick you up and bring you out. You can go back and assume your position as God's creation. If God had wanted man to be a woman, He would have made him one. If He had wanted woman to be a man, He would have made her one. But since He made us what we are, we should accept His wisdom and stay what we are. You say, "I was born that way." That's a lie and a trick of the devil because I know the God I serve. He can get inside you, and He can regulate your organs. He can get inside you, renew your mind, and turn you around. I don't believe God has such folks in Heaven. I believe He can deliver you. He can save you, and He can make a new creature out of you. "Therefore if any man be in Christ, he is a new creature: old things are passed away; behold, all things are become new" (2 Cor. 5:17).

> **Thus saith the Lord, Let not the wise man glory in his wisdom, neither let the mighty man glory in his might, let not the rich man glory in his riches: but let him that glorieth glory in this, that he understandeth and knoweth Me, that I am the Lord which exercise lovingkindness, judgment, and righteousness, in the earth: for in these things I delight, saith the Lord.**
>
> **Jeremiah 9:23-24**

Verse 23 tells us what not to glory in. We are not to glory in our own wisdom, not to glory in the fact we know what to do. We ought not glory in our own might, nor in our own strength. We shouldn't glory in riches because a tornado can come and carry it all away. What should we glory in? Let's glory in the fact that we understand and know the Lord. Let's glory in the fact that we are God's masterpiece. Ask the Lord what He wants you to be and give Him the glory. When God made us, He made us for His glory. He made us to praise Him. That's why the Bible reads, "Let every thing that hath breath praise the Lord…" (Ps. 150:6). One of the quickest ways to get joy in your soul and to start magnifying the Lord, is to lose sight of yourself. Lose sight of your problems, lose sight of your impossibilities, and start magnifying the Lord. Also, when you magnify the Lord, look like something that magnifies Him. When you begin to magnify God, He sheds His light in you. When you begin to give God the glory out of your life, He stands on His jasmine throne and looks over the parapets and the battlements of glory.

When you begin to magnify Him, tell Him, "God, You're amazing! God, You're astounding! You are beautiful! You are magnificent! You are brilliant! You are delightful! You are excellent! You are acceptable! You are fabulous! You are extraordinary! You are glorious! You are grand! You are great! You are incredible! You are marvelous! You are remarkable! You are splendid! You are sublime! You are superb! You are supreme! You are terrific! You are tremendous! And You are wonderful!" When you magnify God and say, "You are the God of my faith; You are going to get the glory out of my life and You are going to have Your way in me," then God moves to meet your needs. He asks, "What do you want Me to do for you? Do you need any money? Do you need healing?" He created you to be an instrument of praise for Him, to glorify Him. If there is anyone who should praise God, it ought to be mortal man.

The angels desire to look into the redemption God has provided, but God didn't die for the angels. God didn't send His Son to Calvary for the angels. The angels haven't been redeemed. Thank God I've been redeemed. I've got a song to sing that the angels can't sing: "I've been redeemed, I've been blood-washed, I've been washed in the blood of the Lamb. He bought me, He paid the price, I belong to Him." When I walk in the church or the grocery store, I throw my shoulders back. I'm His masterpiece. I'm royalty and a member of His chosen generation. I'm a royal preacher and a part of His holy nation. I'm a peculiar person, His product, and I've got His Spirit in me. I can't help acting like Him because He put Himself in me when He blew His life in Adam's nostrils. There's a part of me that walks with Him. There's a part of me that talks with Him. There's a part of me that worships Him. There's a part of me that loves and lives for Him. I belong to Him, and He belongs to me.

Regardless of our physical appearance or what others may say about us, we are God's masterpiece, the crown of His creation. You and I are made in the image of God and no devil in hell can take that from us. We are children of the King. We are His, and He is ours. From the man in the White House to the alcoholic in the gutter, we are all God's masterpiece. Get up. We are the crown of His creation. It is time to wake up, get up, shave, brush your teeth, and get yourself together. Man is designed to be a master. You can master those habits that are causing you problems. You can overcome the things that are hindering you. You can exchange the heavy yokes for the easy yoke of Jesus. Go to your family and say, "I'm going to be what God made me, the head." Look at your wife and tell her, "Honey, you are the queen of this house and I am the king. We are one in Him and we are His masterpiece. We are the crown of His creation."

Begin to Know God

Through Christ Jesus we have received God's salvation. When we know and accept that He has saved us, we will begin to enjoy the fruits of a better life in Him. Genesis 15:1b says, "Fear not, Abram: I am thy shield, and thy exceeding great reward." The Lord will give grace and glory; no good thing will He withhold from those who walk uprightly before the Lord (see Ps. 84:11). Is this true, or was God lying? He said it, and I believe it. Because I can trust Him and because I'm God's masterpiece, healing is in the will, forgiveness is in the will, eternal life is in the will, joy is in the will, and peace is in the will. When Jesus died, the will went into effect. When He rose from the dead, He did not change the will. The will is still in effect. Salvation is in the will. Restoration is in the will. Victory is in the will. You can count on His will and be glad. Now is the time for you to know and accept who you are. You are an heir with God and a joint heir of Christ. You are one of the King's kids. And, because I belong to Him, I've got some more coming. I can always tell in my spirit, even from my preaching, when there is going to be a great deliverance and miracles. If you are a sinner or a backslider, He will reinstate you. He will restore you. He will save you. Today is the day of God's compelling power. The Spirit of God is pulling on you. The Spirit of God is saying, "Come." He is calling to all those who would hear, who are thirsty for Him. Come and drink freely of the water of life.

Chapter 2

Man: God's Crown

As God's crown, men should always enjoy a close relationship with God. In earthly relationships, when you deal with someone who is close to you, a wife or a brother or a sister, it is not too difficult to realize when he or she is upset with you. This is also true with God. Your spirit and His Spirit seem out of sorts, and God's Spirit does not seem to be flowing in your life. This is usually because you have done something wrong and He is displeased or He is grieved. Similarly, when there is genuine fellowship with Him, you know it because of the way you feel in your spirit. You know there is nothing between your soul and the Savior.

Becoming One Spirit With God

In Genesis chapter 3, we read that Adam heard God's voice calling to him (see Gen. 3:8). Before Adam and Eve sinned, they enjoyed a unique fellowship with God. They knew His voice and enjoyed His presence in the Garden. From the time of Adam's fall, God had a plan for man to reestablish this fellowship with Him. The plan was fulfilled through the life, death, and resurrection of Jesus Christ.

There are seven priorities every Christian should know and understand in order to walk as one with God's Spirit. Before we can improve our relationship with those around us—our family, our friends, and our neighbors—we must first establish a good relationship with God. We can begin by accepting the seven priorities outlined below.

Priority 1: The first and greatest commandment is to love the Lord your God with all your heart, soul, mind, and strength (see Mk. 12:30). You must settle His place in your life on the basis of this commandment.

Priority 2: You must love your neighbor as you love yourself (see Mk. 12:31). Jesus said this is the second greatest commandment. When you fail to acknowledge your neighbor and treat him with love and respect, you grieve the heart of God and make void His power in your life.

Priority 3: You must recognize that Jesus is the Lord of your life. He sits at the right hand of the Father in power and He offers this power to you. In the life of every Christian, there is a cross and a throne. Either Christ is on the throne and reigning as Lord in our life, or we have put ourselves in His place.

Priority 4: To maintain your relationship with God, you must *keep Jesus on the throne* in your life. Often people accept Him as Savior, but they won't allow Him to rule in their lives. Often they are only Sunday Christians, living for themselves the rest of the week. Jesus wants to be more than our Savior.

Priority 5: You must make a conscious effort to seek His will for your life. Most of the time we act as if Jesus were not even here. It is important to acknowledge His presence in our life. This means that we must consider Him and what He has to say about the decisions and choices we make.

Priority 6: In all that you do, you are to please God. When you take time to buy a present for your wife or your children, do you consider whether the present will please them? Of course you do. You must also seek to do things that are pleasing to God. You can be sure that you are pleasing God by doing His will. When you try to do things your own way without considering His way, you do not please God. Hebrews 11:5 tells us that Enoch walked with God and by faith he was translated, that he should not see death. Enoch's body was not found because God translated him. Enoch pleased God. Often you must choose between pleasing God and pleasing those around you. If you stay in His will and do what He calls you to do, He will take care of the rest.

Priority 7: You must set aside time every day to fellowship with God. This means that you must talk with Him, listen to Him, and obey Him. Too often people shoot off a fast prayer and think they have done their duty in talking with God. But He wants your full attention. He wants you to take time to let Him know your needs. He also wants you to thank Him and praise Him for the good things He has done on your behalf.

We must please Jesus, acknowledge Him, love Him, know He is the Lord and the boss of our lives, keep

Him on the throne and ourselves on the cross, and maintain our fellowship with Him. When you are born again, you become one in spirit with the Lord. First Corinthians 6:17 says, "But he that is joined unto the Lord is one spirit." When you are joined to the Lord, you are one spirit with Him.

When you are joined to God in the spirit, you enjoy a spiritual union in the spirit that is like a marriage. Unlike marriage, you will never be separated from God, not even by death. Even though your body ceases to function, your spirit continues to live. You may be absent from the body, but you will be alive with Christ. Too often we want to substitute our own plan for God's plan. When we forsake God's way to follow our own, we break our fellowship with Him. We can't have it both our way and God's way. God's way is the best way.

One Flesh in Marriage

After God had formed woman from the rib of Adam, Adam said, "This is now bone of my bones, and flesh of my flesh: she shall be called Woman, because she was taken out of Man. Therefore shall a man leave his father and his mother, and shall cleave unto his wife: and they shall be one flesh" (Gen. 2:23-24).

Just as we are joined to God in the spirit, so is man joined to woman in marriage through the flesh. Marriage was instituted by Jehovah God in the Garden of Eden during the state of man's innocency. Throughout the ages, marriage has been approved and encouraged.

Man: God's Crown

Moses gave marriage legal sanction and the Lord Jesus Christ gave it spiritual sanction. Marriage was designed to be the highest and happiest of human relationships.

Jesus is the first priority in our life. When we are married, our spouse becomes the second priority in our life. Just as Jesus comes before any person or any thing, our spouse comes before mother, father, brothers, sisters, boss, landlord, or any other human being. I don't care how close another person is to you spiritually; your companion comes first *after* Jesus.

God could have made Adam a eunuch, but He saw it was not good for man to live alone (see Gen. 2:18). God could have made Adam so he would be satisfied to live alone, but He didn't. So God decided to make Adam a helpmeet. A helpmeet is someone who would correspond to and fit Adam in every way. God made a suitable helper, one who would be a complement and a counterpart to him. Adam's helpmeet became his partner, companion, and a mate after his own kind. Husbands and wives are supposed to complement one another in words, in deeds, and in expression.

When God took a rib from Adam to make Eve, I am convinced He must have taken the rib closest to Adam's heart—and that made it a prime rib. God could have said, "Adam, do you see all these animals around here? You named each and every one and you can have whichever of these animals you want for your companion for life. Just choose the one that really turns you on and you can have that one to live with and to sleep with for the rest of your life."

Fortunately, God didn't do that. Instead, He decided to make something special for Adam, something that was like him, after his own kind, and therefore, in the image and likeness of God. When God made woman, He made her unique, unlike anything He had created thus far. He made a loving, tender, and compassionate person. When God brought her to Adam, he knew he wasn't looking at anything he had seen before. He knew he had already named all the animals and he must have thought, "Did I miss this one? She's not made like any animal I have seen. She looks like me, yet there is something special about her." That is why he said she was bone of his bones and flesh of his flesh. Adam knew that he was incomplete without Eve.

Man Is the Head of the Wife

> Wives, submit yourselves unto your own husbands, as unto the Lord. For the husband is the head of the wife, even as Christ is the head of the church: and He is the saviour of the body. Therefore as the church is subject unto Christ, so let the wives be to their own husbands in every thing. Husbands, love your wives, even as Christ also loved the church, and gave Himself for it; that He might sanctify and cleanse it with the washing of water by the word, that He might present it to Himself a glorious church, not having spot, or wrinkle, or any such thing; but that it should be holy and without blemish. So ought men to love their wives as their own bodies. He that loveth his wife loveth himself. For no man ever yet hated his own flesh; but nourisheth and cherisheth it, even as the Lord

the church: for we are members of His body, of His flesh, and of His bones. For this cause shall a man leave his father and mother, and shall be joined unto his wife, and they two shall be one flesh. This is a great mystery: but I speak concerning Christ and the church. Nevertheless, let every one of you in particular so love his wife even as himself; and the wife see that she reverence her husband.

Ephesians 5:22-33

It is clear in this passage from Paul's letter to the Ephesians that the husband was given the position as head over the wife. What men often don't realize is that this position, once accepted, must also be respected and maintained in the same way that Christ respected and maintained His position as Head of the Church. When a husband fails to fulfill his duties and responsibilities as head of the wife, he is no longer worthy of his position.

How should the husband fulfill his role as head of the wife?

The first thing Paul tells the husband to do is to "love" his wife and "give" (sacrifice) himself for her just as Christ loved the Church and sacrificed Himself for it. When a man and a woman are joined in the flesh, they become as one. Anything that tends to disrupt the union of the two is like tearing flesh off your body. It hurts and leaves a scar that is often difficult to heal.

How can the husband fulfill his role as a loving and giving partner? Paul says that the husband is to sanctify the wife. This means he is to set her apart from all other women and make her his one and only companion and partner. Men face a multitude of temptations where women are concerned. There are too many opportunities today for men to stray into unholy relationships. If the husband is to truly be the head of the wife, he must set an example of holiness that she can follow.

The husband must also cleanse his wife with washing of water by the word. Women are no more perfect than men. They must be reminded of their duties and obligations to the husband and the family. So long as this comes from the head in love, the woman will be willing to receive instruction and correction. To be the head does not give the husband the right to be the boss. The head controls the body with love. He does not coerce the body by acting like a boss who is the superior partner. The words that will cleanse the wife are words of encouragement, thankfulness, and praise. A husband must be sensitive to the nature of the woman and offer her words that will build her up and not tear her down. When the husband uses positive words to reinforce his wife, he will find that she will become a woman without blemish or spot, just as the Church Christ is building.

Another aspect of the head's responsibility is to nourish and cherish his wife. Exodus 21:10 tells us that a husband is responsible for food, clothing, and marital relations. I believe Paul was thinking of this verse from Exodus when he wrote the verse in Ephesians. You nourish your wife when you provide for her, when you make sure there is money for food and clothing and the other material needs of your family.

You cherish your wife when you fulfill your obligations as her lover by making sure she is your one and only partner in sexual relations. There is more to your job as her sexual partner than simply accommodating her from time to time. As a husband, your responsibility is to make sure she is fulfilled. That means you must be as concerned for her satisfaction as you are for your own. Paul says, "So ought men to love their wives as their own bodies. He that loveth his wife loveth himself" (Eph. 5:28).

The Husband Is the Provider

Paul, writing to Timothy, said, "But if any provide not for his own, and specially for those of his own house, he hath denied the faith, and is worse than an infidel" (1 Tim. 5:8). Times are hard and the job market is tough now. The problem lies in trying to get everything we want instead of concentrating on the things that are needed. When times are hard, you must concentrate on provision rather than on extravagance. Also today, with many couples, both partners are working. This is fine so long as the wife agrees to help out. If as a couple you have set your sights high, both partners may have to work. The important thing is for you to agree and then to work together toward a goal. You may want to take precautions against pregnancy during the early years of marriage. It is better to prevent a pregnancy than to deal with children who are not wanted.

When your goals are achieved, you can reevaluate your situation and decide together how to proceed.

Maybe you can begin to think of starting a family. This may mean the wife needs to quit work or change her work hours to have more time at home. You may have to reduce your standard of living to accommodate the new additions to the family. This is the kind of responsible planning that pleases God and reduces the obstacles that face a growing family. If you don't set some goals, and if you fail to plan properly, you will end up buying big cars with no garage and a two-room house for you and your three children. The problem is that your values are all wrong. You haven't made provision and the Bible says you are worse than an infidel.

The husband is responsible. That is why the Lord rebuked Adam, even though Eve ate the fruit first. God held Adam responsible and the sin was imputed to him. As the head, he was responsible to God for the commandment Eve broke. Adam tried to push the blame off on Eve, but God would have none of his excuses. Do you try the same thing today? When you fail to live up to your responsibility, do you try to put it off on your wife? Whether you try to blame your wife or the devil, the fault is yours.

Honor the Weaker Vessel

Peter, in his first letter, offers additional instruction to the husband. "Likewise, ye husbands, dwell with them according to knowledge, giving honour unto the wife, as unto the weaker vessel, and as being heirs together of the grace of life; that your prayers be not hindered" (1 Pet. 3:7).

When you take time to know and understand your wife, you will not try to make her into something she is not. Comments like, "I wish you were more like Nancy or Betty" demean your wife and send her the message that you do not consider her as valuable as other women. Help her become all she can be as she is. God made her who she is, and she has the capacity to become all that God wants her to be as a woman and as your wife.

Too often a husband will criticize his wife's shortcomings rather than encourage her with God's Word. Women are more aware of their weight or their looks than you are. If you "ride" her about it, you create an opportunity for conflict and anger. Even if a wife needs to lose weight, you don't need to keep reminding her. Once the desire to lose weight gets in her spirit, she will say, "I'm getting this weight off me." Then that is the time for you to encourage her, but not by trying to make her feel small or feel bad about her condition. Deal with your wife according to knowledge.

Peter also says to give honor to your wife. She is your wife, a part of you, one flesh with you. Don't take her for granted. I remember one occasion my wife, Carolyn, dressed up special. She was doing it for me and she was looking to me for recognition. It is the little things that mean a lot. This is showing honor to your wife. You open her car door. Let her enter the room before you. Hold her chair for her and offer her first choice of the cut of the meat. To be thoughtful in the little things is often more important than an occasional big thing.

In the marriage the woman is physically the weaker vessel, but together you are both heirs of the grace of life. You and your wife are heirs of God and joint heirs of Christ. Peter says that when the husband fails in his responsibilities, his prayers are hindered (see 1 Pet. 3:7). It's not your wife's prayers, but your prayers. You can't treat her badly and criticize her and expect God to answer your prayers. You haven't dealt with her as a weaker vessel, and you haven't acknowledged her and given her honor. Don't act like she doesn't even exist when you are out in public. When you belittle her or ignore her, it grieves the Lord because He is looking upon both of you as He does Christ and the Church.

The kind of harmony that comes from such a loving relationship will bear fruit for the husband. His wife will want to dress to please him, cook to please him, clean to please him, and run the house to please him. All this comes because the husband respects his wife enough to follow the blueprint God has laid out in His Word.

Chapter 3

Woman: Helpmeet and More

Although Adam was created first, then Eve from the rib of Adam, Eve was no less a masterpiece of God's creation. Too often we assume the word *helpmeet*, as applied to Eve, implies that woman is less than man. That may be because we have come to view a helper as a sort of apprentice and not fully vested with the same abilities as the one who is being helped. Again, to take this view is to misunderstand what is meant by the word *helpmeet*.

Over the years pastors and preachers have applied a variety of meanings and interpretations to this word, often resulting in great injustice to women in general and wives in particular. To understand what the word means in Genesis 2:18, we need to know two things: (a) the word *helpmeet* is a translation of two Hebrew words; and (b) the original Old English meaning of this word and the meaning of the Hebrew words are very close to the same thing.

The two Hebrew words *ezer keneghdo* literally mean "an identical helper." If we look in a good English dictionary, we find the meaning for helpmeet to be "companion, partner, co-worker." The implication is not one who has less ability, but one who has abilities that complement the one she is helping. In the same way, the man has abilities that complement his helper, the woman. In this sense, both the man and the woman are "helpmeets," since each one fits the other and fulfills an important role in the relationship.

Now you can see what Peter meant when he said, "giving honour unto the wife, as unto the weaker vessel" (1 Pet. 3:7). You honor those who support your weaknesses with their strengths, when you supply them with your strength where they are weak. Paul offers us the flip side of this in Ephesians 5:33 when he says, "...and the wife see that she reverence [honor] her husband." The man is due honor from the wife because of his position and the woman is due honor from the husband because of her position.

One writer, commenting on Genesis 2:18, said that when Adam inspected and named all the species of animals, he found that some were indeed suited to serve and help him to some extent. But, in the end, he could find no one animal that was his "like" (this is the Hebrew word *keneghdo*). As a result, the writer continued, Adam became conscious of his loneliness and yearned for one who could be his life-companion and a helper fit to be his soul-mate (*ezer keneghdo*) in the full sense of the word. If Adam could only have such a person in his life, he would be ready to appreciate and cherish the gift that the Lord God was to give him.

When Adam saw Eve for the first time, he was overwhelmed with her. He knew immediately that she was all that was missing in his life. He knew that she was bone of his bone and flesh of his flesh and, in accepting her as his wife, they became one flesh together.

The Priorities of a Wife

If I were to ask you to list the priorities of a wife, you might begin with children, home, cooking, cleaning, and so on. All these are things that fall under the duties and responsibilities of a wife, but they are not priorities. Let me list a few of the most important priorities for us to consider.

Priority 1: As a woman and as a wife, her first priority is Jesus Christ. The wife who will build a solid faith in Jesus Christ and seek to do His will in her life, will be empowered to endure and overcome the hardships of life. To place Jesus first is to build a firm foundation and to release a wellspring of living water from which the wife can draw comfort, love, and knowledge.

Priority 2: As a wife, her second priority is her spouse. It is important that a woman choose her husband-to-be carefully. What happens with a man in the heat of the moment may not be a true picture of life day in and day out with him. In the cooing and wooing stage of any relationship, everyone looks good, smells good, tastes good, and feels good. In the bright light of the early morning, you may be faced with an unshaven face and bad breath. The Bible assumes that the spouse you choose will be yours for life. Since your husband will be your first priority after Jesus, you should be sure that you are willing to commit yourself to him for life. Paul says, "And unto the married I command, yet not I, but the Lord, Let not the wife depart from her husband" (1 Cor. 7:10).

Priority 3: As a child and heir of God, the wife is also a joint heir of the grace of life (see 1 Pet. 3:7). Although the inheritance God has provided for us is given freely, we are not supposed to take it lightly or squander His blessings. The wife, along with the husband, has a responsibility to maintain honesty and integrity in the home. Paul ended his first letter to Timothy by saying, "...O Timothy, keep that which is committed to thy trust, avoiding profane and vain babblings, and oppositions of science falsely so called: which some professing have erred concerning the faith..." (1 Tim. 6:20-21). The wife must be ever watchful and diligent for her husband and her home, or the devil will use every opportunity and every weakness to destroy the marriage.

Priority 4: In First Corinthians chapter 7, Paul tells us the wife is sanctified by the husband and the husband is sanctified by the wife. In this way the children are also sanctified or made holy. Often a woman will marry a man who is not a believer. He doesn't come to church and does not uphold godly values in his life. According to Paul, the unbelieving husband is sanctified by the wife. The temptation is great to give into the ways of the world in dealing with a troublesome man.

The wife must work hard to maintain her faith in God and to bring that faith into action at every opportunity in the marriage. One of the ways this can be achieved is through prayer. Just as the fervent prayer of a righteous man will produce results (see Jas. 5:16), so too the fervent prayers of a faithful wife will preserve and strengthen a marriage.

Priority 5: Once the husband and wife decide to start a family, the wife often shifts much of her attention to the children. This is natural and understandable. Although the husband must be sensitive to the changes in his wife as she moves into motherhood, the wife should not neglect her responsibilities as a wife. For all the love and care she will need during the term of pregnancy, she must not allow her new child to take the place of her husband. It is important for her to communicate her love and concerns to her husband so he will feel a part of the process rather than a bystander. Since sexual relations will be at a premium during the latter stages of pregnancy, the wife must find ways to replace this most intimate of times with special occasions where they can be alone together.

Priority 6: After a child is born, the first few years of that child's life will be a time where the care and learning comes almost exclusively from the mother. The Book of Proverbs confirms the mother's role in instructing the child in good moral values during the first few years of life. Soon, the father will take over and provide the discipline and ethical values that will carry the child into adulthood. The wife and mother must be prepared to impart wisdom, compassion, and understanding to the child. These will form the foundation that the child will draw upon for the rest of his life. It is also important that the wife consult the husband in matters concerning the children so the parents do not work at cross purposes. As the head of the wife and the leader of the family, the husband and father is ultimately responsible to God and must agree with the way in which values are being taught.

The wife who is willing to embrace these priorities in her marriage will be sure to succeed. She will enjoy more intimacy with her husband and find that she is becoming more of what God wants her to be as a wife and mother as each day goes by.

The Role of the Wife in the New Testament

The wife has a responsibility to do everything in her power to make the marriage work. Often this is difficult, especially if the husband is not a believer. In Ephesians 5:22, and also in Colossians 3:18, Paul says to the wife, "Wives, submit yourselves unto your own husbands, as unto the Lord." Men have used this verse to beat women into submission and to put them in a lower category than the husband. What we often fail to see is the end of this verse: "as unto the Lord."

God did not intend the wife to be a slave in her own home. Rather, she was to be a soul-mate, an equal partner, and a supportive companion. Her role, then, is to help the husband achieve his potential as a provider, lover, friend, and father. As he lives up to his responsibilities of loving his wife, honoring his wife, nourishing and cherishing his wife, and sanctifying and blessing his wife, the wife is to respond by submitting to him as her head. That does not mean he is the absolute boss over her. Remember, the head is to control by leading in love and not by coercing.

There are four motives in marriage: physical pleasure, material advantage, social prestige, and rearing children. Some of these are easier for some people than for others. The husband who is a workaholic may be able to give his wife every material advantage, but the hours he works may not allow much time for family and social functions. Such an obsessive worker may also find little time for physical pleasure. The wife must assess the qualities and strengths of her husband and help him strengthen the things he does well and help him develop and improve the things he does not do well. By submitting to him in all areas, he will learn from her willingness to forgive his shortcomings and from her encouragement and support.

Physical Pleasure: There is no doubt of the importance of physical pleasure in a marriage. The two major causes for divorce are lack of money and lack of sexual satisfaction. Fornication and adultery are rampant in society today, but they occur most often where a wife or a husband fails in their sexual responsibilities. Paul says:

> **Let the husband render unto the wife due benevolence: and likewise also the wife unto the husband. The wife hath not power of her own body, but the husband: and likewise also the husband hath not power of his own body, but the wife. Defraud ye not one the other, except it be with consent for a time, that ye may give yourselves to fasting and prayer; and come together again, that Satan tempt you not for your incontinency.**
>
> **First Corinthians 7:3-5**

The wife's appearance is particularly important. If you wives will be truthful, you know you feel better when you look good. Well, you are also more desirable when you look good. If you are always in curlers or an old terry cloth robe when your husband comes home, his mind may begin to wander. He is faced with a lot of women on the job, on the streets, on the bus, or in restaurants, who are dressed well and are after a man. You can make sure he won't stray if you give him a reason to do all his sampling at home. Find a way to get the children out of the house from time to time, take the phone off the hook, turn off the TV, prepare an intimate supper, put on some special lingerie, turn down the lights, and let nature take its course. An occasional evening centered around you and your husband will do wonders for your marriage and your relationship.

Material Advantage: Every husband wants to give his wife a nice place to live and nice things to enjoy. In the past much of the wife's contribution to the material side of marriage was in the home as a cook, seamstress, maid, teacher, and mother. These jobs are still important, but modern technology has taken a lot of the pain out of the process. There are many things that help relieve the strain, but they all cost a lot of money. The old wood-burning stove has been replaced with microwave ovens and fast-heating ranges, but they are expensive. One of the roles the wife may have to assume is one that makes her a part of the income stream.

Many families cannot enjoy the benefits they desire with only the husband's paycheck. If the wife decides to work, the decision should be made and agreed to by both partners. The wife should understand that the husband may be reluctant to do more around the house even though she may need him to help out. This should be discussed and each party should understand what is expected of them. There is much reward from two incomes, but there is also a lot of pressure because there is less time in the relationship. This pressure increases when children are a part of the equation. Nevertheless, if the wife will work with the husband in setting down realistic goals for the material side of marriage and work with him to reach these goals, the process can succeed.

Social Prestige: Every wife likes to be recognized in her community as a person of character and integrity. She wants to have a husband she can be proud of and children who are well-behaved. Too often social prestige is measured by how much money you have, how well you dress, or how big your car is. The true measure of social prestige is how much you give back to your community of your time, talent, and treasure.

For most Christian families, the center of their social world is their church. A wife who takes time to give of her time and talent to her church community will always be held in high esteem by those who are around her. By giving of herself, she also brings honor to her husband. Proverbs 19:14 says, "House and riches are the inheritance of fathers: and a prudent wife is from the Lord." *Prudent* means a careful wife, a discreet wife, a cautious wife, a thoughtful wife, a skilled wife, and a thrifty wife, one who is not extravagant. Such a woman will insure that her family will be accepted socially by the community.

Rearing Children: No one can think of a wife or of marriage without thinking of children. The Bible considers children a blessing from God. The first few chapters in the Book of Proverbs deal with the way in which a mother influences the life of her children. Not only does she carry them in her womb, she also births them in pain and rears them with the wisdom that only a mother can possess. Often the mother has the advantage of more time with the children than the father, especially if she is at home during the day. It is important for the wife and mother to be aware of all the evil that lurks outside the house so she can prepare her children for the worst. Drugs, alcohol, sex, and money are ever-present temptations that face children every day on the street and in school. It takes a mother with strong values and a determined will to keep her children on the path that leads to a godly life. To be less than vigilant can cause your children to face a life of addiction, disease, jail, and even death. Failure is certain where parents don't care at all about their children.

Men often get all puffed up with pride over their accomplishments in business or in sports or as a husband and father, but I am sure nothing they feel can compare with the joy of being a wife and mother. Though the job is tough and often without much recognition, there is no job in the world more important. I am sure God gave women the hardest part because He knew they were more than capable of handling the position.

Chapter 4

The Virtuous Woman

Who can find a virtuous woman? for her price is far above rubies. The heart of her husband doth safely trust in her, so that he shall have no need of spoil. She will do him good and not evil all the days of her life. She seeketh wool, and flax, and worketh willingly with her hands. She is like the merchants' ships; she bringeth her food from afar. She riseth also while it is yet night, and giveth meat to her household, and a portion to her maidens. She considereth a field, and buyeth it: with the fruit of her hands she planteth a vineyard. She girdeth her loins with strength, and strengtheneth her arms. She perceiveth that her merchandise is good: her candle goeth not out by night. She layeth her hands to the spindle, and her hands hold the distaff. She stretcheth out her hand to the poor; yea, she reacheth forth her hands to the needy. She is not afraid of the snow for her household: for all her household are clothed with scarlet. She maketh herself coverings of tapestry; her clothing is silk and purple. Her husband is known in the gates, when he sitteth among the elders of the land. She maketh fine linen, and selleth it; and delivereth girdles unto the merchant. Strength and honour are her clothing; and she shall rejoice in time to come. She openeth her mouth with wisdom; and in her tongue is the law of

kindness. She looketh well to the ways of her household, and eateth not the bread of idleness. Her children arise up, and call her blessed; her husband also, and he praiseth her. Many daughters have done virtuously, but thou excellest them all. Favour is deceitful, and beauty is vain, but a woman that feareth the Lord, she shall be praised. Give her of the fruit of her hands; and let her own works praise her in the gates.

Proverbs 31:10-31

The above passage from Proverbs has been quoted time and time again as the standard for the perfect woman. Of course, there are no perfect women. Fortunately, women don't have to try to live up to each and every quality listed here. Through Christ Jesus, they are free to be the best they can be and no matter how far short they fall, God will neither forsake them nor leave them without His love and blessing.

This passage is valuable, however, as a basis for learning how to be more like the woman God would have you to be. Each of the qualities enumerated here are food for thought and a goal to work toward. The passage begins with the question, "Who can find a virtuous woman?" In this sense, the word *virtuous* means "strong in moral and mental qualities." It is interesting that the next sentence tells us the value of such a woman: "For her price is far above rubies." Today we would say such a woman is "priceless."

How many women do you know who are priceless? Do you consider your mother or your wife priceless?

The Virtuous Woman

You only realize the price of something when you need it and you don't have it or can't afford it. That is true of a wife or a mother. They do so much to make life in the home easier that the husband often takes them for granted. That is why Paul told the husband to honor the wife.

It costs something to be a woman. It isn't easy submitting to a husband who does not appreciate your efforts. It is often difficult to offer love and care to children who constantly demand more and more from you without so much as a "Thank you, Mom." Husbands and children everywhere should take time to consider the quality of their life because they have a caring woman as a wife and mother. Then, they should find a way to honor her with the appreciation she is due.

I am not sure the women who champion the women's lib movement would agree with me, but I believe motherhood is the highest and best calling of any woman. There is little doubt that women are frequently underpaid in the job market, but that is changing. It seems the attitude in the workplace is shifting toward greater recognition for women. At the same time, I do not believe women have any place in the trenches during a war, and neither do I think they look so good doing construction work. Their talent and energies should be directed to more productive and less hazardous occupations.

In reading and teaching the Bible, we seldom dwell on the contribution made by women. Rahab, the harlot, saved her family and helped God's chosen people in the battle for Jericho—and was included among the faithful of Israel. Ruth left her own people and followed Naomi back to Israel after the death of her first husband. From Ruth and her husband, Boaz, came the line of David, which produced Jesus, the Messiah. Hannah, the prophetess, gave her son, Samuel, to the Lord and proclaimed, through prophecy, that the anointed one would come.

In the New Testament, we have numerous references to women who made valuable contributions to the work of the Messiah. After the disciples had fled in fear and despair, women anointed Christ's body with spices and fragrant oils. It was the women who returned to the tomb on resurrection morning to discover the tomb was empty. It was a woman who carried the news to the disciples, who were in hiding and who considered the news nothing more than idle tales. A few of the women of importance include Elizabeth, Eunice, Herodias, Priscilla, Martha, Mary, and Mary Magdalene. Most, if not all, of these women were also wives and mothers. They gave of their time and their talent to the cause of Christ while, at the same time, they discharged their duties to their husbands and their families.

Set Free in Jesus

Most people think women's lib is a new thing, but you should know that women were liberated 2,000 years ago by Jesus. "There is neither Jew nor Greek, there is neither bond nor free, there is neither male nor female: for ye are all one in Christ Jesus" (Gal. 3:28). Jesus didn't liberate women to look like men, walk like men, and do what men do. He set them free to enjoy the fullness of God's Kingdom and His blessings for their life.

Before Jesus came, women were considered to be like pieces of furniture and put in the category of livestock. In the Ten Commandments the last commandment says, "Thou shalt not covet thy neighbour's house, thou shalt not covet thy neighbour's wife, nor his manservant, nor his maidservant, nor his ox, nor his ass, nor any thing that is thy neighbour's" (Ex. 20:17). In other words, the wife was thrown in with the ox and the ass, but when Jesus came, He liberated the woman.

Consider the woman caught in the act of adultery in John 8. She couldn't commit adultery by herself; a man had to be involved too. Nothing is said about the man because women did not have the same rights as men at that time. The man could just go and change his clothes as if he had done nothing wrong, while the woman was left "holding the bag." According to the law, she was to be stoned. When confronted by her accusers, Jesus did nothing more than write on the ground as He said, "He that is without sin among you, let him first cast a stone at her" (Jn. 8:7). Jesus didn't say not to stone her; He only gave them a chance to consider their own sinful condition. When Jesus looked up and asked the woman where her accusers were, she said there were none.

God's Masterpiece

Then Jesus told her that He didn't condemn her either. He set her free from the penalty of the law. At the same time, He did not condone her sin. He told her to go on her way and sin no more.

Jesus was demonstrating a new freedom for women and the way they should be treated. He liberated Mary Magdalene when He cast seven devils out of her. Mary the sister of Martha honored Jesus and anointed His head with precious perfume. Under the old law, women were not supposed to approach men. They were treated as nothing more than servants. In Old Testament times it wasn't whom you loved, it was whom you wanted. Which one of these girls do you want? "Eenie, meenie, miney, moe." The woman had nothing to say about her choice of a husband. That's the way it was in Old Testament times, and the same custom continues in many parts of the world today.

In Christ Jesus women have been set free. Wherever the gospel has been preached throughout the world, women have been liberated. How are they accepting this new freedom? With compassion, modesty, and humility? No, they are not satisfied with simply being a woman. They want to be like a man. God carved out a place for women and they should stay there. Our society is messed up because everybody is out of place. The man wants to be the woman, the woman wants to be the man, the children want to boss the parents, and everything is all out of whack.

The Virtuous Woman

With the virtuous woman, "the heart of her husband doth safely trust in her, so that he shall have no need of spoil. She will do him good and not evil all the days of her life" (Prov. 31:11-12). A virtuous woman will support her husband and help him become what he's supposed to be. A virtuous woman doesn't talk about her husband behind his back and then sleep in silence with him every night. Marriage takes a lot of adjustment and a lot of compromise. But marriage and lives given over to Jesus can be greatly enhanced.

The Qualities of a Wife

> **She seeketh wool, and flax, and worketh willingly with her hands.**
>
> **Proverbs 31:13**

Too many women are not willing to work today. In times past the woman had to bake bread, scrub and wax floors, and do the laundry by hand. Today life seems to be instant this and instant that. The priority is to put personal pleasure ahead of the house and the family. As a result, chores go undone or jobs are not sought outside the home. It is easier to rely on the government than to set goals and improve the situation.

That is not to say that all women are in this rut. Many do work outside the home and contribute financially to the family. Not all women are sluggards when it comes to housework either. These women should be acknowledged for their work ethics. They are close to the biblical model of the virtuous woman.

> **She is like the merchants' ships; she bringeth her food from afar.**
>
> **Proverbs 31:14**

There are several verses in addition to the one above that relate to the role of the virtuous woman as one who is wise when she shops. This woman in the Old Testament must have travelled far to get the best food at the best prices for her family. A woman who is thrifty is a woman who can be trusted. The husband doesn't have to worry that his paycheck will be spent unwisely. The other verses (see verses 15, 18, 19, 22, and 24) speak of the woman weaving, sewing, selling, and cooking. As verse 27 says, she "eateth not the bread of idleness." A woman who wants to see her family taken care of is not one to sit by and leave things undone. Today, we would call such a woman determined and industrious.

> **She considereth a field, and buyeth it: with the fruit of her hands she planteth a vineyard.**
>
> **Proverbs 31:16**

This is an interesting verse and one that speaks of a quality a woman has that we often fail to give her credit for. We know that women generally have the ability to know a good buy when they see it. This ability often leads to good judgment in finding bargains in property and other investments. A wise husband will consider his wife's opinion and listen to her counsel when it comes to major purchases. A woman's insight and foresight give her a solid vision for the future of

The Virtuous Woman

her family. Women should not discount these innate qualities and waste their time in frivolous matters that are not productive.

> **She girdeth her loins with strength, and strengtheneth her arms.**
>
> **Proverbs 31:17**

No man can do the things a woman does with ease—baby crying, doorbell ringing, talking on the phone, cooking dinner—and she handles all this at the same time. A man would go insane trying to keep up with his wife. Every woman has a source of strength that is unique to the female. It is not the same physical strength of the man, but is more a strength found in endurance and determination. No one is better suited or capable of doing the jobs required in a household than a wife and mother.

Deborah: Wife, Prophetess, Judge, Leader, and Mother

In the fourth chapter of the Book of Judges, the story of Deborah unfolds. Deborah was the wife of Lapidoth, but the Bible tells us nothing of her husband except his name. She is unique among the judges because she was a woman and a prophetess. According to the text, she is the only judge of Israel who actually judged (see Judg. 4:5). Because she was a woman of great wealth, she dispensed justice without remuneration. She was also an able leader during the time of war. This war between Israel and the Canaanites may have been the last war between these two peoples. It was her wisdom and cunning that enabled Israel to defeat this mighty foe. The victory in this war was a woman's victory. Not only did the woman, Deborah, lead and command the troops, but another woman, Jael, actually killed the commander of the Canaanite army. In the annals of history, Deborah stands out as a great national leader.

According to the historians, Deborah, Hannah and Mary are three women of the Bible who composed praises to God unequaled by those written by men (see Judg. 5; 1 Sam. 2:1-10; Lk. 1:46-55). As women of God, all these women are examples of faithful servants who sought to do God's will and who were rewarded with blessing and prosperity in their lives.

In her song of praise to God, Deborah tells us she "arose a mother in Israel" (Judg. 5:7). In other words, she stood up and took the place God had prepared for her. How much better would the world and the Church be today, if women everywhere would rise up and assume the role God has prepared for them? Too often women are trying to take someone else's place and so miss the call of God for their own life. For Deborah, it was not enough to be a judge or a prophetess—she was destined to nurture and care for the whole nation as a mother would for her own children.

We seldom refer to women in our church as "mothers" today. I suppose we figured it isn't found in the New Testament, so we don't use it. Well, there are a lot of words that aren't found in the New Testament that are used in the Church every day. We need mothers in the Church, mothers who exercise authority, who teach their daughters. Mothers who are mature in their faith and show wisdom in their life should have a place as an elder in the church.

The name, Deborah, means "bee," a honey bee. In the society of honey bees you have three classes: queen, drone, and worker. The queen lays the eggs, the drone tends to and fertilizes the eggs, and the worker gathers food and keeps and protects the hive. Each bee knows its own place in the society. When a bee becomes isolated or fails to return to the hive, it dies. So long as it stays with the other bees, it can live for years. Within the society of the hive there is strength, unity, and productivity. You will remember the old saying, "busy as a bee."

Bees are determined to do their work. Every one is working to get the job done. Bees are the only insect that produce food eaten by man. It is said that the queen bee does not rule the colony, but is the force that holds them together. She doesn't rule the beehive, but she has the ability to hold everything together. Isn't that just like a mother? If mothers would only realize the power they have, they could change the world. I don't care how big, robust, and strong a fellow says he is, he can't stand up to the power, strategy, and wisdom of his mother. I don't mean trying to stand toe to toe and play the man's game. There are so many other ways and strategies that will get the job done.

For example, gambling is available on the Chicago River in the new casino ships. At any one time, the ships are filled with husbands who have no business squandering the money the family needs for food and clothing. If the wives and mothers of these men would simply get together and march on the casino, you would see a fast exodus of men down the ship ramp.

If wives and mothers would get together, they could stop the gangs that threaten their neighborhood. Fifty or a hundred mothers banding together in a common cause can get a neighborhood cleaned up. It is happening here and there, but not often enough. Mothers know what their sons and daughters should be doing with their free time. Let them know that you and the other mothers are not going to put up with the drugs and alcohol and stealing and shooting anymore. March into the gang headquarters 50 and 100 strong and tell them to close it up or get out. You might think, "I could never do that. I am not strong enough to confront these gang members." I am not saying you should do it alone. I am saying you should band together, work together, and find ways to become a force to be reckoned with in your neighborhood and your community.

No one can pray like a woman. No matter how much a man moans and groans in prayer, he will pray for 15 or 20 minutes and then he is through. A woman can pray all night. A woman will pray until she gets an answer to her prayer. She won't give up. Like the Syrophoenician woman who persisted in prayer at the feet of Jesus, a determined wife and mother will hold on to the hem until the answer comes. It is time for women to rise up as never before with conviction and faith and be strong mothers in Jesus' name.

Chapter 5

Marriage in the Will of God

Most people get married—some more than once—but how many couples do you know who are genuinely happy with their marriage? As a pastor I often counsel men and women as they prepare for marriage. Some of the marriages are solemnized by me. Some are solemnized by others. What disturbs me, though, is the number of divorces that are occurring not only among those in my church, but also in society as a whole. The divorce courts are jammed with case after case. Marriage counselors are enjoying a banner business. The situation has become so critical that some social scientists are seriously questioning whether the institution of marriage will survive.

In the wake of so many failures, many men and women are experimenting with other kinds of relationships. Countless conceivable relationships, which they consider alternatives to marriage, are growing at alarming rates. Men and women are forming "partnerships" that are not based on anything other than a loose commitment. Still, in the face of what seems to be overwhelming odds at a successful marriage, I believe marriage is the most sacred of unions and was designed by God to work. You see, the problem is not with the institution of marriage as God intended, but with the people involved. For the most part they have no idea how marriage is supposed to function.

Of course, there is no lack of information on how to succeed in marriage. All you need to do is go to the nearest bookstore or library and you will find volume after volume detailing all the "how to's" of marriage. Marriage is a hot topic, as evidenced by the numerous articles in magazines and television talk shows. The computer matchmaker services have become a major industry, offering anyone who will subscribe to their service the opportunity to find the "perfect mate." It would seem that this proliferation of information would result in more success than we are experiencing. I would like to suggest the major reason we are seeing so many divorces, and so many marriages having so much trouble, is a failure to look in the right place. We need to return to the "Manufacturer's Handbook" and take a look at the origin of marriage. I believe we will find that marriage is God's will for every man and woman who desires an intimate relationship.

Marriage the Bible Way

The biblical record will show that when God created man and woman, He intended them to be *one* in marriage. The way this is to take place and the way it is to succeed is found in His "Handbook." Some who read this book may be an unbelieving partner in marriage or may simply discount anything to do with godly practices. Everyone has the gift of free will and they are free to choose whatever method suits them. But I am convinced there is little or no chance for happiness in marriage without God in the center of the relationship. There is a spiritual side to marriage, and then there is a natural side. If you want to enter into marriage God's way, you must first find out what God requires. If you do decide to go your own way, that is up to you, but don't do it in God's name.

Marriage is under satanic attack today. It's not just marriage that is under attack, but also the home, the children, the whole family structure. Satan has a definite plan and has brought all his evil ways to bear in an effort to destroy this institution of God. He knows if he can destroy the unity that exists in a godly marriage, he will also have destroyed a mighty force for righteousness. In Ephesians 5:31-32 Paul says, "...they two shall be one flesh. This is a great mystery...." The bond between man and wife represents a powerful bond that is a "great mystery." The force behind this spiritual secret can actually bring the devil trembling to his knees. He is powerless when confronted by a man and woman who hold fast to the union God has glued together. The devil has not given up the fight. He is bringing to bear on solid marriages more and more social, financial, moral, emotional, and spiritual pressures.

There is still time for you to make a quality decision about your marriage. It is not too late for you to change the problems you face into solutions. All that is required is for one of you to revise your way of doing business in your marriage and to renew your mind through Christ Jesus to God's way. God will work with one of you or both of you. Of course, it takes less time if both are involved, but God will accept whichever partner is ready to learn how to pump new life into a marriage. If you are the one God is calling, you must be ready and willing to listen to Him. I don't mean you must simply open your ears, but also your heart and mind. You must be ready to change as God gives you course corrections. Begin by having faith that God will honor your willingness and rest assured that you will see positive results almost immediately.

The Origin and Nature of Marriage

I want to return to the Book of Genesis and God's first words concerning marriage, and then I want to reinforce it with a couple of passages from the New Testament.

> **And the Lord God said, It is not good that the man should be alone; I will make him an help meet for him. ... Therefore shall a man leave his father and his mother, and shall cleave unto his wife: and they shall be one flesh.**
>
> **Genesis 2:18,24**
>
> **...For this cause shall a man leave father and mother, and shall cleave to his wife: and they twain shall be one flesh? Wherefore they are no more twain, but one flesh.**

> **What therefore God hath joined together, let not man put asunder.**
>
> **Matthew 19:5-6**

> **Art thou bound unto a wife? seek not to be loosed. Art thou loosed from a wife? seek not a wife.**
>
> **First Corinthians 7:27**

There is another way to look at the importance of these three passages: Woman was created to meet man's needs and when they are married, the two are no longer two people; they are to become one person. (See Ephesians 5:22-31.) The passage from Genesis makes plain God's intention—He wanted man and woman to come together to form a holy union, a union set apart by Him. This union was and is to be a witness of God's will to society.

When Jesus repeated His Father's will in Matthew's Gospel, He was stressing the permanent nature of marriage as God provided in His original plan. Paul, in writing to the early Church, consistently repeated this same viewpoint. The early Church was filled with non-Jews who were abandoning pagan practices to take up the cross of Christ. They were accustomed to multiple wives, orgies, and all sorts of ungodly sexual practices and relationships. Paul, as the teacher of the Gentiles, made God's will clear concerning the responsibilities of marriage.

The pews are filled with men and women who can give testimony to the power of God in rejuvenating their marriage and making whole again that which had fallen apart. Some of these testimonies come from men and women who have been going to church for years, but who never listened to God's will for them. Others come from men and women who have recently given their life to Jesus Christ and have experienced, for the first time, the joy of oneness as they both submit their relationship to God. What was a marriage made in hell has become a life together in God's heavenly Kingdom.

When a marriage begins to fall apart, too often the partners turn to divorce as the only answer. Divorce brings with it anger, pain, and suffering, and is seldom the answer to the problem. Divorce is nothing more than temporary relief from an inner sickness. It is like trying to treat the symptoms of a disease instead of the disease itself. In the end these same partners often end up in another relationship and, eventually, another marriage. The chances for success in the second marriage are often no better than those for the first. The same personalities, the same conflicts, and the same problems emerge time and time again. It is like a whirlpool from which there is no escape.

The world offers psychiatric solutions to the problem. Couples enter sessions based on conflict resolution. They discover a multitude of reasons for their failure: in-laws, finances, sex, religious differences, personal oddities, selfishness... The list is too large to complete. The problem is that man is trying to fill a void that can only be filled with Jesus Christ. His basic animal drive for food, sex, and self-defense is not nearly enough to satisfy his craving for more. He also needs love, companionship, and feelings of self-worth. All these are unavailable apart from God. Without God in their marriage, all that a man or woman will discover is the most shallow of substitutes, if they seek to find them in the world.

Choosing a Mate With Care

Most divorces could be avoided if each mate would consider his or her choice carefully. Too often the decision to marry is made in the heat of the moment. Or, the family may be putting pressure on you to get a husband or to get a wife. They say, "You know you aren't getting any younger. Pretty soon you will be too old to have children." You should never agree to marriage because someone else thinks it is good for you. Take your time and choose your mate with the conviction that this is the one person you want to live with for the rest of your life. It is better to spend a year or more dating, than to have a quick wedding and find out that you have made a mistake.

Remember Paul said that once a woman is married God's way, she must not leave her husband (see 1 Cor. 7:10), and the husband must not put away his wife (see 1 Cor. 7:11). Even if the wife does leave, she is to remain unmarried or be reconciled again to her husband. That is why it is so important for Christian women to consider marriage and their mate carefully before they take that step. This is the Christian way in marriage. To fail to obey God's Word is to act like a heathen. There is no such thing as no-fault divorce in the Body of Christ.

If a believing husband and wife drop their guard, the devil will find a way to tempt them. Usually, he brings another person into the relationship. Jealousy and lust are two of the most powerful tools of the devil. In Hollywood, every time you turn around someone is getting a divorce. They are giving into lust, and there is something about the spirit of lust that never offers you fulfillment. When a husband leaves his wife or when a wife leaves her husband, they think they are gaining their freedom. But where lust is involved, no man or woman will please you. Lust is a spirit that is never satisfied.

Communication Is Important

You can usually judge how well a husband and wife communicate with each other by how well they communicate with God. If your prayer life is nonexistent, your conversational life with your spouse is also nonexistent. A marriage founded in Christ and put together by God presupposes an active prayer life. When problems arise, take them first to God. As the head, the husband is responsible to God first. This is where he is to submit his will. Except for grace at meals, too often the husband waits for the wife to initiate prayer. Prayer should be at the top of his agenda. He should pray before beginning a serious discussion, before they go to bed, and when they get up in the morning. He should also find time to bless his wife and thank her for the care and affection she shows toward him. Paul, in ending his letter to the Ephesians, says, "Praying always with all prayer and supplication in the Spirit, and watching thereunto with all perseverance and supplication..." (Eph. 6:18).

A marriage that is dedicated to God is a marriage filled with abundant life. The devil and the world will lie to you and tell you that religion is dull and boring. They will tell you that marriage is too restricting, especially if it is lived under the constraint of God's law. Any marriage can be a drag if you make it so. But Paul tells us that this is not the way of a marriage filled with the Spirit of God. He tells us to be wise in the way we walk with God and we will live our life not drunk on wine or drugged the world's way. Rather we will be filled with the Holy Spirit and live a life of soberness and joy.

> **See then that ye walk circumspectly, not as fools, but as wise, redeeming the time, because the days are evil. Wherefore be ye not unwise, but understanding what the will of the Lord is. And be not drunk with wine, wherein is excess; but be filled with the Spirit; speaking to yourselves in psalms and hymns and spiritual songs, singing and making melody in your heart to the Lord; giving thanks always for all things unto God and the Father in the name of our Lord Jesus Christ; submitting yourselves one to another in the fear of God.**
>
> **Ephesians 5:15-21**

These few verses are filled with power-packed suggestions for having a marriage filled with joy and peace. The key to good communication in marriage begins with prayer and continues as you speak to one another as Paul has prescribed. When you work at your marriage God's way, you won't have time for anger and resentment. You will deal with your differences and go on to greater heights. Your meals will taste better, your conversation be more enjoyable, and your sexual encounters more fulfilling. God makes the incompatible, compatible; the mundane, exciting; and the impossible, possible.

Chapter 6

Making Marriage Work

The last time I reviewed my basic math skills, one plus one did not equal one. Still, according to God's math on marriage, this is good arithmetic. You may say this can't be so, but then some pretty smart men once said man would never fly. I will always side with God. After all, He created man and woman to begin with. He should know what is best for His creation. It is like the company that manufactures automobiles today. When the car becomes damaged or worn, the company has certain instructions that tell the mechanic where to look to solve the problem. They tell the mechanic what parts to replace and what sort of performance standards to expect from a properly functioning vehicle. The same is true with God's plan for marriage. He is more aware than you or I am of the hazards a couple will face as they adjust to each other and overcome obstacles to a happy marriage. When something is missing, He knows what to add to the process or to eliminate from the process. Whatever God requires, you can rest assured that the end result will be a smooth-running marriage.

God's Masterpiece

One thing is for sure: no man or woman is an island. This means they are not complete without a relationship of some kind. When you look at the personality of any human being, you will find that it is incomplete. There is something missing. That is why the world's way will not work in marriage. There is a spiritual side that can only be supplied by God, and for God to be in the equation, you must follow His plan. If you are having problems in your marriage and you have tried everything you know to fix the problem, you should stop trying your way and try God's way.

I know there are a number of people who will say this is not true, that they have a happy and fulfilled life, that they are not trying to follow God's ways. What they don't understand is that there are degrees of happiness and degrees of fulfillment. With God there is no falling short of the mark. With Him in your marriage, you will realize God's ultimate blessing for your life and your marriage. Although you are inadequate by yourself, you become completely adequate when you are joined to your spouse in Christ Jesus. Without your spouse, you are trying to run with half your spark plugs missing. When you meet your mate, you will suddenly realize that you have been missing some parts. When they are put into operation, you become a unified, functioning couple.

Have you ever noticed that it is usually opposites that attract? Often at the end of the first year of marriage, after the honeymoon is long past, you will find the man in one room praying, "God, please change that woman," while in another room the woman is praying for God to change that man. Although you may think you and your wife will never fit together and become one, you are really different halves of the same piece. It is like a piece of wood that has been broken. Each side has jagged edges where the break occurred and each broken edge is different from the other piece. But when you apply some glue and put the two back together, you find that they fit perfectly. In spiritual unions, such as marriage, Jesus is the glue that holds the pieces together. Paul confirms this when, referring to Jesus, he says, "And by Him all things consist" (Col. 1:17b).

Working Together as One

If we recognize that we are incomplete and inadequate without our mate, we suddenly take a giant step toward creating solutions for many of the problems we face in marriage. For instance, money is one of the primary sources of disagreement in a marriage. One partner may spend too much and the other may be too frugal. Sometimes both are spendthrifts. The constant pressure of meeting bills and making payments on time leads to conflict. Still, one partner is generally more adept with finances than the other. If it happens to be the wife, the husband often refuses to release the checkbook for fear that he will lose his position. What he needs to do is recognize his wife's ability and let her deal with the checkbook. That way they will always have enough to cover the necessities.

Another big issue is children and discipline. Often one partner will be too lenient, while the other will be too strict. As the parents battle over the proper way to resolve the issue, the children are the ones who endure the damage. Again, it is time to make an adjustment, to reach some sort of balance in the marriage. This is particularly true where one marries into a ready-made family. If the man has three children or if the woman has three children, each one has to assure the other of their love and devotion. You cannot make the husband or the wife feel like every choice considers the children first. The woman and her three children can't join together and take sides, making the husband feel like an outsider. Simply because these are children of your first marriage doesn't give you the right to forsake your responsibilities to your husband or your wife. A husband can't afford to make his wife feel like nothing more than a maid or a cook. It is important to realize that issues concerning children are often the cause behind marriages that fail.

Consideration and communication are important, and there is no dishonor in compromise. Although the husband may fear he will end up henpecked by a strong-willed woman, or the wife fear she will be smothered by a dictator-like husband, the best place to end up is in the middle rather than too far to one side or the other. With Christ Jesus as the glue and love as the motivation, what could be an opportunity for divorce will be turned into a lifetime of happiness. As long as one partner insists the other change, the relationship will be in conflict and the marriage in trouble. Once they realize that God doesn't ask either one to change, only to make a spiritual adjustment, the marriage will begin to move from two separate and incompatible persons into one indivisible flesh.

When the husband discovers his wife has everything he needs to be complete and adequate as a man, and when the wife realizes that in her husband she has everything she needs to be complete and fulfilled, the pieces will slide together with ease. The broken edges will fit together perfectly. Married life is not unlike the car I described earlier. A car needs periodic checkups, oil changes, engine tune-ups, and so forth. The same is true of a marriage. Oneness is not achieved instantly. It takes prayer, time, and adjustment. One of the biggest problems is the closeness of the husband and the wife. The needs of each partner are related in such a way that they are almost impossible to separate. Without God in the equation, neither partner is willing to make the necessary adjustment and thus, they miss the ultimate blessing God had in mind when He established marriage as the highest and best union.

Working on Becoming One in the Flesh

How do you make two stubborn personalities become one? When we turn to First Peter, chapter 3, we find these words: "Likewise, ye wives…likewise, ye husbands…." The word *likewise* is the key to the way this section on marriage is introduced. To find out what is happening here, we need to look again at chapter 2.

This is where we find what the husband and the wife are supposed to emulate.

> **Servants, be subject to your masters with all fear; not only to the good and gentle, but also to the froward. For this is thankworthy, if a man for conscience toward God endure grief, suffering wrongfully. For what glory is it, if, when ye be buffeted for your faults, ye shall take it patiently? but if, when ye do well, and suffer for it, ye take it patiently, this is acceptable with God. For even hereunto were ye called: because Christ also suffered for us, leaving us an example, that ye should follow His steps: who did no sin, neither was guile found in His mouth: who, when He was reviled, reviled not again; when He suffered, He threatened not; but committed Himself to Him that judgeth righteously: who His own self bare our sins in His own body on the tree, that we, being dead to sins, should live unto righteousness: by whose stripes ye were healed. For ye were as sheep going astray; but are now returned unto the Shepherd and Bishop of your souls.**
>
> **First Peter 2:18-25**

When Peter continues in chapter 3, he is saying that just as a servant is to submit to both good masters and harsh masters; and just as Jesus Christ did not attack those who condemned Him, but was patient in bearing the suffering for our sakes; so too, or just like this, are husbands to dwell with their wives. To put it another way, the husband is to stick by his wife when she is nice and loving as well as when she is unkempt, lazy, and nagging. At the same time, or likewise, the wife is to submit to her husband when he is good and considerate and when he is crude, demanding, and controlling.

There are many wives who agree they are to submit to their husbands, but they appeal to Paul's version in Ephesians 5:22 and Colossians 3:18, where the verses end "as unto the Lord" and "as it is fit in the Lord." Too many wives have used these words as a way out of submitting to their husbands. They argue that this means they only have to submit when their husbands obey God. Of course, this makes Christian wives, who have unbelieving husbands, the judges, and it gives them the freedom to determine when their husbands live up to their concept of marriage. Fortunately, this is not what Peter and Paul meant and these women are simply playing with God's Word. It will help us understand what the apostles meant if we look more closely at Paul's verse from Colossians 3:18:

Wives, submit yourselves unto your own husbands, as it is fit in the Lord.

Colossians 3:18

If you read this verse with an open heart and mind, you will see that a wife who willingly submits herself to her husband is doing a "service" unto the Lord. This means that the way a husband responds to God or fails to respond to God has nothing to do with the wife's responsibility. The question for the wife is, "Will you do what God wants you to do?" That is the question that must be decided. Once a wife has accepted God's way in marriage, He will take charge and establish order if order is needed, or change if change is needed.

> **Likewise, ye wives, be in subjection to your own husbands; that, if any obey not the word, they also may without the word be won by the conversation of the wives.**
>
> **First Peter 3:1**

It should be clear that Peter is trying to make the wife understand what her attitude toward her husband should be. If she is cantankerous, resentful, cold, or petty, she is grieving the Spirit of God and blocking His action in her life. The marriage will continue to be chaotic and there will be no opportunity for change. Peter describes the way the wife is to act in her role as the submissive partner.

Did you realize wives are supposed to *enjoy* their husbands? This is only possible when the wife truly turns her life and her marriage over to God. Once she realizes how miserable she is in her marriage and how she has failed on her own, God will move in and cause her to change. Then she will be able to enjoy her husband.

As Christians, we should understand that we are totally dependent on God. No husband can be the head of his wife without submitting to and being dependent on Christ; likewise, no wife can submit to her husband and be dependent on him in her own strength. God, through Christ Jesus, can tear down the barriers fear has built between a wife and her husband. God can mold her heart and mind so she no longer asserts selfishness and independence. In their place He will plant and nurture love and joy and fill her with strength and resolution.

Sarah: Wife in Submission

When we study the story of Abraham, we often fail to realize it is also the story of Sarah. We tend to focus mostly on Sarah's age, her barrenness, and her age at the time of Isaac's birth. Since husband and wife are one in the eyes of the Lord, we should take time to consider the contribution of each partner. Obviously, there is more information on Abraham, but what we know of Sarah is no less important. Abraham was, of course, known as the "father of the faith." Have you ever considered that Sarah should be known as the "mother of the faith"? Peter has something to say about Sarah in the same passage we have been using as a reference for the role of the wife in marriage.

> **Even as Sara obeyed Abraham, calling him lord: whose daughters ye are, as long as ye do well, and are not afraid with any amazement.**
>
> **First Peter 3:6**

You may think that any woman who could be married to a man with such great faith as Abraham would have it easy. Not only had God called him righteous, but He had made him the father of Israel. Still, Abraham was only human and he was subject to the same problems and temptations that you and I experience. Whereas Sarah should have been at peace in her relationship with Abraham, the Bible tells us there was a time when she failed to trust her husband and almost gave in to fear. To understand her fear and to realize that her faith was often greater than Abraham's, we have to look at Genesis 12:10-20.

In this passage a famine has forced Abraham and his family to journey to Egypt. When they arrived in Egypt, Abraham is concerned that his wife's beauty might attract the Egyptians. But his concern was not for her safety—it was for his. He feared that they would try to kill him and keep her alive for themselves. He convinced Sarah to tell the Egyptians that she was his sister. Of course this put Sarah at risk, since, as his sister, she was fair game for other men. Sure enough, her beauty was noticed and she was taken to Pharaoh, but the Lord intervened and sent a plague on Pharaoh's house. Pharaoh confronted Abraham with his lie about his wife and sent them both away without harm to Sarah.

When Abraham asked Sarah to deceive the Egyptians, she could have argued with Abraham and called him a coward for looking after his own skin at her expense. Instead, she obeyed Abraham's request and put her trust in God. The story doesn't tell us what happened when she was taken from her husband and led off to the palace of Pharaoh, but she must have fallen on her face before God to remind Him of His promise of protection. She must have reminded Him of her obedience to her husband and the way she had submitted to his request. In answer to her prayer, God visited Pharaoh as he waited with expectation for the latest addition to his harem. God caused a series of plagues and Pharaoh must have realized something was wrong.

When he learned that Sarah was Abraham's wife, he had his answer. When he confronted Abraham and demanded an answer for his deceit, Abraham must have replied, "I was afraid...."

Pharaoh also saw that Abraham was a man of God, so he let him and his family go with all their livestock and goods. Sarah came out of this whole mess unharmed. She could have decided she would not submit to Abraham in this case. It doesn't take much faith to submit only when you feel like it or when your husband is at his best. When your husband is strong, manly, filled with God's Spirit, and otherwise living up to your every expectation, submission is easy. What we learn from Sarah's actions is she submitted to Abraham even when she knew he was wrong. In submitting to her husband, she was also obedient to God and, therefore, she was protected from all harm.

Would she have been justified in refusing to obey Abraham? Had she refused, she would have been disobedient along with Abraham and the problem would have been greater than it was. Sarah trusted God with her fear instead of Abraham and God moved to bring her out of certain danger. God can and will work in your marriage just as He worked in this marriage thousands of years ago. Either you can let God fight your battles or you can fight your own battles. How far should you go in submitting to your husband? You should submit as much as your faith will allow. Your faith in God is the deciding factor. Sarah was not afraid of the consequences of Abraham's act. She knew that by submitting to her husband, God would move to defeat any enemy that would raise his hand to harm her.

God Is Faithful

God is faithful even when submission doesn't seem to be working for you. If you are not experiencing the fullness of God's promise for your marriage, the basic problem may be you are following the letter of the law, but without the right spirit. God is not fooled by false or selfish motivations. He wants you to turn everything over to Him. He doesn't want you to submit as an exercise that you are going to try for a while. He wants you to experience a permanent change in your attitude, which will allow Him to take your fleshy heart and fill it with His Spirit.

You can begin by settling some things in your mind once and for all times. I want to list these as a sort of checklist. You can use them as a reference from time to time to check up on your spiritual condition. I am sure you will begin to see dramatic changes once you allow these truths to guide your actions.

1. Regardless of what you think or what the devil tries to get you to think, God's law has not changed. He has not changed His mind for you; neither is He wrong in what He requires of you.

2. When you are faced with apparent defeat, take a step back and reexamine your priorities for submission. Make sure you are not trying to be

manipulative or entertaining yourself with a pity party or trying to be a martyr in your efforts.

3. Don't forget you are to submit to your husband, but you are first to submit unto God in faith. This means you must truly believe He will intervene on your behalf and turn the seemingly impossible into the possible.

4. You must also realize that you are taking a great risk in releasing so much authority. Sometimes the husband will not accept your submission to him. When you see this is the case, you must be even more sure of your trust in God, especially where children are concerned. Remember, Paul said, "...having done all, to stand" (Eph. 6:13).

5. Finally, don't lose sight of your goal: submission to and enjoyment of your husband. When there is no evidence that your submission is working, you must reexamine the spirit of your submission. Obviously, more work needs to be done on your part.

Chapter 7

Likewise You Husbands

The subject of submission is so sensitive and so hard to get across, we often spend more time discussing this issue than any other in the marriage process. This doesn't mean men are privileged characters or something. They are accountable for their behavior as much or more so than the woman, even if they are not actively involved in putting God into their marriage. It should be some comfort to the wife to know that God will not allow an irresponsible husband off the hook. God can and will deal with every husband to bring about His will and to complete His purpose and plan for their life and for their marriage.

Once a woman makes a quality decision and submits to her husband, God is free to deal directly with the husband. If the wife refuses to obey God, she is like another obstacle in God's way. Or if she makes up her mind to take care of her husband her own way, she becomes an even bigger obstacle. She is like a catcher at home plate, blocking the way so the runner cannot score. God doesn't want to knock her down to score, so He waits patiently until she decides to get out of His way.

All this becomes clear when you consider the whole concept of marriage. God took two opposites, or two different bodies, one a man and the other a woman, and joined them together to make one complete body that was better than the two He started with. In any body, there is only one head, and the Bible is clear about who is to be the head of the married body.

> **But I would have you know, that the head of every man is Christ; and the head of the woman is the man; and the head of Christ is God.**
>
> **First Corinthians 11:3**

According to this verse, the pecking order is like this: the wife is responsible to her husband, her husband is responsible to Christ, and Christ is responsible to God. Now you can see why Sarah could be sure of her safety in submitting to Abraham even though he was wrong. God stands at the top of the ladder and He takes full responsibility for us. Because He loves us, He covers us like an umbrella, protecting us and guiding us as we go along the path with Him. As long as we stay under His covering and submit to the one who is our head, He will not allow us to be harmed.

In the previous chapter, I made the statement, "Oneness is not achieved instantly." On the other hand, headship is bestowed instantly, at the moment the two repeat their marriage vows. It is a fact that a couple grows into oneness day by day, but a husband does not grow into headship. Whatever a man is and whatever he does with what he is, God invests the husband in his position from the moment the marriage is consecrated. Unfortunately, the man does not always know he is supposed to be the head of his wife, their body, their home, and their family. One reason most husbands don't realize their responsibility is they do not see other husbands acting like the head of their respective wives and families. It makes no difference what husbands do or fail to do, God has set the order in motion and He will not change His mind.

Any wife who is sitting around waiting for her husband to become spiritual enough for her to submit to as her head is wasting her time. He is what he is, regardless of his mental, emotional, physical, or spiritual condition. Can you see why it is so important for men and women to consider their choice of partners with care? Once you have said the final "I do," the only way to ensure success in marriage is for the husband to be head and the wife to submit to him as her head. You can trust God, though, because He has a way of making sure the man knows where he stands.

Most husbands like the submission side of the equation. They use the Bible as a means of getting what they want by saying, "Wife, you are supposed to obey me!" Before you husbands get so full of yourselves, you had better read the next verse: "Husbands, love your wives…" (Eph. 5:25). Paul says this is a great mystery and you can be sure the devil wants to keep it hidden. It is important that husbands pray for God to open their understanding so that they can do what is required of them.

> **Husbands, love your wives, even as Christ also loved the church, and gave Himself for it; ... So ought men to love their wives as their own bodies. He that loveth his wife loveth himself. For no man ever yet hated his own flesh; but nourisheth and cherisheth it, even as the Lord the church: ... Nevertheless let every one of you in particular so love his wife even as himself; and the wife see that she reverence her husband.**
>
> **Ephesians 5:25,28-29,33**
>
> **Wives, submit yourselves unto your own husbands, as it is fit in the Lord. Husbands, love your wives, and be not bitter against them.**
>
> **Colossians 3:18-19**

Christ is not only the head of the husband, He is also the example or pattern the husband is to follow (see 1 Pet. 2:21). That means the husband must not only do what Christ does, but he must also carefully observe how He does it. Again, Peter gives us direction in this area when he says, "Likewise, ye husbands, dwell with them [your wives]..." (1 Pet. 3:7). He said that servants or slaves are supposed to obey their masters whether they are good or bad to them, for this is the example Christ established. This same example is applied to marriage, and the wife must submit to her husband, whether he is good to her or not. Similarly, the husband is not free to love only when the wife is sexy, sweet, and kind. The husband is to love his wife regardless of how unloving she may be.

In what way is the first requirement of the husband carried out? How does Christ love? As a husband, you can begin by putting aside your weapons of defense and destruction. When your wife needles you, you don't retaliate. When your wife nags you to take out the trash or fix a broken pipe or stop looking at all the pretty girls, don't snap at her. Return her distrust, misunderstanding, and hostility with a powerful dose of love.

Once you get the picture and realize that God is taking two stubborn, independent personalities and molding them into one whole person, you will begin to experience the wonder of oneness. Like two pieces of precious metal in the refiner's fire, God will slowly separate the dross, scoop it off the top, and leave the pure metal behind. As you husbands begin to understand the great responsibility God has bestowed upon you and the awesome authority He has conferred upon you, then you will start to see your desires fulfilled.

You say, "Man, that is hard to accept with all this women's lib today. How are we going to get women to submit to us? They will take us to court for sexual harassment." It is true the women of today are trying to change their role in society. Their propaganda machine is working full-time educating women, boys, and girls to think like them. For a hard-nosed women's libber, men are a necessary evil and have no use beyond copulation. They want everyone to look alike, think alike, and act alike. They want marriage to be nothing more than a mutual agreement between two equal, but independent and responsible people. How can we overcome such a closed mind-set?

The answer lies in Christ Jesus. Through Him we are more than conquerors and more than able to overcome the lies of the devil (see Rom. 8:37). God's plan and the Bible have withstood attack after attack, century after century, and they are still standing today. You can be sure the world will experience the consequences of going against God's plan. Only His own will be safe in the end.

The whole concept of headship in marriage is so fundamental that it cannot be avoided. It is a principle established by God, and those who refuse to accept His way are doomed to fail. Because many decide to go their own way and establish their own rules, they are destined to a life of chaos and confusion. There is both peace and stability in God's order. Perhaps you can think of a family that has failed to follow God's command and has harvested the bitter pill of defeat in the process. The husband who fails to exercise the authority God has given him is sure to experience the consequence of God's wrath.

God Takes Your Vows Seriously

> **...This is the thing which the Lord hath commanded. If a man vow a vow unto the Lord, or swear an oath to bind his soul with a bond; he shall not break his word, he shall do according to all that proceedeth out of his mouth. If a woman also vow a vow unto the Lord... And if she vowed in her husband's house, or bound her soul by a bond with an oath; and her husband heard it, and held his peace at her, and disallowed her not: then all her vows shall stand, and every bond wherewith she bound her soul shall stand.**
>
> **Numbers 30:1-3,10-11**

Likewise You Husbands

The husband, the widowed, and the divorced are bound by the commandment of the Lord as noted in the first part of these verses. The wife, however, was an exception if she lived in her husband's house. If he so chooses, the husband has the authority to release her from her vow. If he does not release her, the consequences are as follows:

> **But if her husband altogether hold his peace at her from day to day; then he establisheth all her vows, or all her bonds, which are upon her: he confirmeth them, because he held his peace at her in the day that he heard them. But if he shall any ways make them void after that he hath heard them; then he shall bear her iniquity.**
>
> **Numbers 30:14-15**

This is exactly the same thing Paul and Peter were referring to when they covered the headship of the husband. The same principle that is given by Moses at God's command to the people of Israel, is repeated by Peter and Paul in their letters to the Church. This same principle is in effect today.

Wives may not like the result of this commandment from God because it will drastically change their way of life with their husbands. For example, if a wife comes home and tells her husband she has promised to be the den mother at the local Cub Scout troop, or sing in the choir, or serve lunch at the soup kitchen, or walk in a protest march, or join a local women's group, and he thinks she has made a bad vow, he is to tell her so in love. Even if she says, "But, honey, I made this promise to the Lord," God won't hold her to it because her husband is the head. He must give his permission first or his wife is not submitting to him as unto the Lord.

This authority must be administered as Christ would to His Church. Christ never forces His will on His flock. The flock can either obey the Shepherd or rebel. There are consequences either way—blessing or cursing. When the Church fails to obey Jesus, there are dire consequences in store for them. When the wife fails to obey her husband or when the husband fails to treat his wife with love, the consequences of their actions fall upon them individually. Remember, the authority of the husband does not include the right to force the wife to obey. Jesus is the Head of the Church, not the tyrant. The same applies to the husband.

The husband forfeits his position as head of his wife if he refuses to recognize Christ as His head. If he refuses to accept Christ's position in his life, how can he love his wife as Christ loves us? Another mystery Paul wrote about is that Christ lives in each one of us. While Jesus is kind, patient, and compassionate by nature, we are stubborn, demanding, selfish, and unloving by nature. We only act as we should when it helps us to get our way. Headship isn't easy and some men may not even want to be the head of their wife, but unless it becomes a reality in a marriage, the man and his wife will never become one. The marriage and the whole family will not grow spiritually; neither will they mature.

Do you find it easier to act lovingly toward a neighbor or a friend or your co-workers, than to act lovingly toward your wife? Have you ever thought why this is so? Could it be that you have to deal with sticky problems every day with your wife, but all these others are out of sight and out of mind once you part company? When you come home and your supper is burned, or the children are noisy as you try to read the paper or watch the news on TV, you usually exercise your own brand of authority rather than Christ's brand of love. You won't know how to get through the hard times unless you have a strong and consistent prayer life. You must take time from your personal schedule and give God an opportunity to teach you how to be the head of your wife and your family.

First Headship, Then Leadership

If you cannot submit to Christ and assume your proper role as head of your wife and family, you will never be ready to assume a position of leadership outside of the home. God will not promote you to a position of importance with His people if you can't handle the job He has given you at home. Paul covers this in his letter to Timothy:

> **A bishop then must be blameless, the husband of one wife... one that ruleth well his own house, having his children in subjection with all gravity; (for if a man know not how to rule his own house, how shall he take care of the church of God?) ... Let the deacons be the husbands of one wife, ruling their children and their own houses well.**
>
> **First Timothy 3:2,4-5,12**

Both headship and submission are qualities that must be learned over time. They do not come easily, but they can be achieved. Our walk with God must be consistent if we are to ever reach full maturity in the Lord. The husband who yields to Christ is never abusive, and he slowly develops an attitude that enables him to use his God-given authority properly. He is firm, but loving; strong, but not forceful; determined, but not controlling. A husband who has found his place as head of his wife and family will not take advantage of his position or those who look to him for leadership.

The wife of such a man will enjoy him and also be free to enjoy her life. She won't have to worry about her position in the home or in society. She will not find it necessary to demand recognition based on her gender. Everyone whom she comes in contact with, will know without being told that she is a liberated woman in Christ Jesus. A fish is free to be a fish as long as it stays in the water; a locomotive is a workhorse of power as long as it stays on the track. A wife must accept the track she is on and stick to it to reach her full potential as a wife and as a woman.

Dwell With Your Wife According to Knowledge

> **Likewise, ye husbands, dwell with them according to knowledge, giving honour unto the wife, as unto the weaker vessel....**
>
> **First Peter 3:7**

When you read First Peter 3:7, it becomes clear that Peter, in speaking of "knowing" wives, is talking about two kinds of knowledge. One kind of knowledge deals with the marital relationship and the other deals with the wife as a person and her needs as the physically weaker partner. As men, we are notorious for our lack of understanding when it comes to knowing a woman's needs. Seldom are we able to love our wife as she wants to be loved. Sadly, many women are starved for love and sex in their marriage. For the most part, a wife has a sincere desire to please her husband, but God makes the man responsible for initiating love. Remember, women are supposed to submit first and husbands are supposed to love first.

Most women, when questioned, admit they have more to give than they are giving. It is not their fault that they are using only a small percentage of the love they are capable of bestowing on a man. They are sitting by, waiting for their husbands to increase the flow by opening the faucet and letting the full force pour through. Men are so intent on personal satisfaction in all phases of their life that they miss the greatest blessing of all—the power of unrestricted love from their wives. This will only happen when the husband is willing to overlook the obvious and go for that which is hidden beneath. The love inside a woman is like an untapped vein of gold, but a husband will never strike it rich if he continues to focus on her bad habits. He must love her when she cries, or complains, or argues back, or schemes to get her own way. Those occasions when she burns his toast or forgets to wash his underwear or sort his socks are all opportunities for him to demonstrate his love for his wife.

You may say, "I have a hard time understanding my wife now. How can I ever figure out what she needs?" This is where the Holy Spirit comes into the picture. John 14:26 and John 16:13 say: "But the Comforter, which is the Holy Ghost, whom the Father will send in My name, He shall teach you all things..." and "...He will guide you into all truth...and He will shew you things to come." If you are sincere about finding out what your wife's needs are, you will have to be in tune with God. This means you need to ask God to show you her needs. God will show you things about your wife you would never have thought of and could not possibly know. I mean the little things, like walking with her hand-in-hand, or rubbing her back after a hard day, or special ways that turn her on to your advances.

Like the wife, you must be careful that you don't use love to get what you want or to remake your wife into your own image. This is not love at all; it is a perversion of the purpose of love in a marriage. God will not honor selfish motives. Just as the wife is to submit to her husband regardless of his condition, so must the husband love his wife whether he sees changes or not. You need your wife to become one flesh with you, and that is the motivation for your love. This is loving your wife "according to knowledge" and as the process goes on, you will begin to see subtle changes.

These changes are brought about by your love and the response of your wife to your love. Her motivation begins to change and she is not so intent on getting you

Likewise You Husbands

to do what she wants. She is content for you to be who you are and suddenly you begin to realize that you have never been more free than you are now. All the while, your wife is becoming more and more like the wife you envisioned. She will begin to live, not for herself or her children, but to please you. She responds to your love as you reach out to her in love.

Almost every principle of the Bible is based on Jesus' parable of the sower. You are familiar with the story of seed sown on several types of soil. Some of it grew up with weeds, some was taken away by the birds, but the seed that was sown on good soil sprouted and produced its full fruit. Likewise, you must sow love in your wife if you are to reap a crop of enjoyment from her. If you choose to sow neglect or bitterness or resentment, you will get the same kind of crop growing in your marriage. If you plant turnip seed, no matter how hard you try, you will not be able to get blood out of the turnip fruit. You can threaten the turnip, you can bribe the turnip, you can even beat the turnip, but you won't get blood out of it. This is true with your wife too. The more harsh you are with her, the greater the harvest of harshness will be in your marriage. As the husband and head of your wife and family, you decide the type of crop you will harvest. What you do and how you do it affects you, your wife, and your children.

The Bible also tells us that each thing produces its own kind. No crop simply happens. It takes water, fertilizer, cultivating, and care to bring forth a crop. When you sow the seeds of desire and fulfillment, you will reap a wife who is more desirable than you could ever have imagined. She will enjoy you and you will enjoy her for the rest of your lives.

Chapter 8

God Has Even More in Store for You

*I*n the corporate world there is a term often used by personnel managers when they hire new people. They talk about the "perks" or "fringe benefits" of the job. This may be a health plan or a pension plan, or it may be the company retreat, a playground for the employees' children, or a day-care facility. Whatever these additional benefits are, they often play an important part in an applicant's decision to take a job.

God has fringe benefits too. These benefits come when the man and woman apply His principles to their married life and work toward oneness. Two of these benefits are mentioned in First Peter 3:7:

> ...as being heirs together of the grace of life; that your prayers be not hindered.
>
> **First Peter 3:7**

The Blessings of Inheritance

Life is full of opportunities and surprises we will never uncover or experience until we become one as husband and wife. The inheritance God promises here is a joint inheritance and it cannot be enjoyed or experienced by one individual alone. Neither can marriages that have no knowledge of God or any interest in God's ways, experience the benefits of this joint inheritance. God has given a husband and his wife the opportunity to become "joint heirs of life" with Him. The life God has in store for you will move beyond the simple union of man and wife and on to form a communion of souls between the two. Although it is true that this is a spiritual experience, it also affects the fleshly and earthly relationship. Joy and satisfaction beyond our wildest dreams will suddenly become a common occurrence. Some men and women have enjoyed only brief glimpses of this ecstatic realm. In God's plan, this ecstasy is to be the normal way of life.

When does this promised life begin? The door to this life will begin to open when the fighting, friction, resentment, anger, and selfishness stop. This happens when the man begins to love his wife with the love of Christ and when the wife submits to her husband in faith. The unity that occurs in a marriage like this goes against everything the world offers. It conquers a hostile society filled with evil distractions and ungodly actions. It lays waste a life of swinging couples, multiple partners, and gross sexual practices. Such a marriage, founded on God's principles and adhering to God's plan, will stand out like a beacon in a lost and dying world. It will cut through the confusion and chaos and open the windows of Heaven, from which blessings will pour out that no place can contain.

God has blessings available for every aspect of our life. He wants to restore our spiritual nature and bring perfect peace into our soul. He wants to restore our emotional nature so we can be at peace with ourselves, our spouse, our children, our neighbors, our friends, and our boss. He wants to give us physical and financial health so we can enjoy the benefits of His creation. It is a shame to see all of God's creation operating at such a low level. He has a storehouse of resources available to us and He wants to show us how and when to use them.

The Benefit of Answered Prayer

In addition to the many blessings God wants to bestow on us, He also wants to hear and answer our prayers. Answered prayer is another of the fringe benefits God provides to a husband and wife who are living according to His plan. Have you ever tried to storm the doors to the throne room in order to get your prayers heard, and then decide God must not be taking requests that day? If you would listen closely, you would hear the voice of God saying, "Take care of your wife and your marriage first, then I will hear your prayers." I challenge you to give this a try. You will be amazed at the results once you work on becoming one flesh as God demands.

You can hardly imagine the effect this will have on your sex life, your finances, your children, your job—every aspect of your life. As heirs *together*, you have a prayer benefit that will outdistance the best investment you could make. But it won't happen unless you and your wife make it happen. Together you have the power to cause success in your life and in your marriage.

Children Are an Inheritance

> **Lo, children are an heritage of the Lord: and the fruit of the womb is His reward. As arrows are in the hand of a mighty man; so are children of the youth.**
>
> **Psalm 127:3-4**

One of the many blessings of life and marriage are children. As with all gifts we receive from God, there is both enjoyment and responsibility. A parent who fails to cherish the gift of children and fulfill parental duties, opens the door for serious consequences.

> **For I have told him that I will judge his house for ever for the iniquity which he knoweth; because his sons made themselves vile, and he restrained them not.**
>
> **First Samuel 3:13**

Children left to their own devices are sure to stray. Today, unacceptable behavior is often deemed "cool" by a child's peers. Children who can control their parents and avoid discipline for their wrong actions, are often heralded as champions and placed at the head of the gang. Is this the fault of the child? To some extent the answer is "yes," but the real blame lies with parents who refuse to address the problem early and give time to their children as the Lord requires. What is intended as a blessing to a couple will only be enjoyed as a blessing if the children are given guidance, discipline, instruction, correction, and love.

Restless Youth

In Lamentations 2:18-19 we read:

> **Their heart cried unto the Lord, O wall of the daughter of Zion, let tears run down like a river day and night: give thyself no rest; let not the apple of thine eye cease. Arise, cry out in the night: in the beginning of the watches pour out thine heart like water before the face of the Lord: lift up thy hands toward Him for the life of thy young children, that faint for hunger in the top of every street.**

You may have children or grandchildren who are young. Almost everyone, at one time or another, touches the life of a young person. Today we see so many young people who are restless, bored, and unhappy. The hunger referred to in the verses just quoted is not a hunger for a Whopper or a Big Mac. Our youth are going astray because they are trying to fill a spiritual void with material things. It is time we realized we are in a spiritual battle over the life of our children and that it will take a supernatural power to fill their hungry souls.

It will take more than a prayer tossed at God, hoping He will hear it. We are going to have to learn how to lament as the prophet Jeremiah was lamenting for the children of Israel. Some of you would be surprised to learn what your children are involved in every day.

Many have no idea where their children are or what they are doing right now. Children are not dumb. They know how to say the things you want to hear. They are better at playing the role of a good child than you are at being a good parent. The youth of today are faced with more and more temptations, and the sad fact is they are giving into them. They don't know how to resist and they are going down the drain.

Why is there such an effort to destroy the children? I would liken it to the destruction of the dinosaurs millions of years ago. A dinosaur was a difficult animal to kill. They were big and didn't die easily. The enemies of the dinosaurs figured out they could solve their problem if they would only destroy the eggs and not the adults. This is what the devil and his forces are trying to do to our society today. No matter how strong we are, if they can get our children to follow them and their wicked ways, our numbers will slowly decrease and we will become extinct.

Unfortunately, our children don't have role models who are solid examples of Christian principles. If we don't begin to show them the pitfalls they face in the world and give them an example they can follow, they will be blinded by the dazzle of the world. If we wait too long, they will refuse to listen to us and we will not be able to do anything to offset what society is offering them. They will listen to the voice of the world and go society's way. When the Church is not strong enough to hold them, the secular world will pull them in.

The power of God is more than enough to defeat the forces of the devil, but if this battle is to be won, it must be won through us.

> Gather the people together, men, and women, and children, and thy stranger that is within thy gates, that they may hear, and that they may learn, and fear the Lord your God, and observe to do all the words of this law: and that their children, which have not known any thing, may hear, and learn to fear the Lord your God, as long as ye live....
>
> **Deuteronomy 31:12-13**

Are you setting a good example for your children and teaching them reverence for God? Or do they hear you on the phone tearing down first one person and then another with your gossip? Can both blessing and cursing come from the same mouth? They figure the Church is really a glorified Hollywood where everybody is acting and you are at the head of the line playing your part. We are dealing with a new breed of youth who can see right through our hypocritical act. They are no longer laid back, but are demonstrating a new boldness not seen before. They are asking hard questions and demanding truthful answers. If you haven't walked the walk, you cannot talk the talk. They won't be fooled by your words when in your actions you do the opposite.

The world is giving them answers, but they are the wrong answers. At the same time, the churches talk about getting what you want from God instead of getting strong and dealing with the tough issues that face the children. You can prosper and be in hell, while the kids are trying drugs, alcohol, sex, homosexuality, and lesbianism. They are experimenting with every kind of deviant practice and destructive substance because they have no foundation to build upon. We have to educate our children by teaching them God's ways. We have to show them a path to follow so they will know which way to turn when the time comes. Solomon said it like this:

Train up a child in the way he should go: and when he is old, he will not depart from it.

Proverbs 22:6

If there ever was a time we need a real education department in the church world (people who don't just preach sermons, but who will be willing to spend time talking to and teaching the youth), it is now. If parents don't get a good grip on them at home and deal with them at home, they will be lost. It is only a matter of time, for we are dealing with a new breed. You can't keep your children locked up with a ball and a chain. You can't keep them behind bars until you get back from work and then hope they don't give in to the pressure on the streets. Our only hope is to show them the way to salvation, to teach them to love God, and to keep them busy in the service of the Lord.

Our youth don't know how to be grateful for the things they have because we have indulged them and given in to their demands for more. This spirit of ingratitude offers no thanks for what it receives because it assumes a parent is supposed to cater to a child's every wish. As a result, our children give us a guilt trip when we don't respond as they feel we should. We need to turn this thing around, take control of our family, and guide the lives of our children. We need to become the boss again over our children. We birthed them—they didn't birth us. We shouldn't have to work like a bunch of fools to make sure our children have the same toys as the Joneses. We have to stop trying to keep up with the Joneses to please our children. It won't hurt them to go without or to wait until we can afford to buy them a new toy.

Not only are we dealing with restless and ungrateful youth, we are also dealing with youth who are giving in to strong sex drives. Just because they don't come home and discuss their fantasies with us, don't think they aren't out there trying to experiment. This is all part of the process of instruction. We have to deal with the issue of sex early in their life. The schools are teaching sex education to first-grade children. If we take a holier-than-thou attitude at home, the child will see us as old-fashioned and "out of touch." We can't stick our heads in the sand like an ostrich; if we do, when we come up for air, we may find our daughters pregnant or our sons having to marry the girl.

One of the biggest problems a youth faces today is peer pressure. Whether you like it or not, your child is going to find a group that will accept him or her. It is the nature of children to find some group with whom they can fellowship. Either they find that group with your help or they will find it on their own. It is important for you to be involved in the process. You should meet the family of the children your child is hanging around with. If you start early, you can steer them in the right direction. If you fail to get involved, they may end up in a gang. They are being driven by peer pressure in the neighborhood, in the schools, and on the playground. The devil makes them think that they have to please their peers and that they have to compete for approval from the group. If you have laid a proper foundation, they will know how to respond when they are faced with difficult choices. When they are called square or chicken because they won't smoke a joint or take a swig, they must have some value planted in their mind. They must know that all they have to do is pick up the phone and call their parents for a ride home. The parent must be prepared to respond to their cry for help without condemning them. Be glad they had enough sense to call. Don't jump down their throat because they put themselves in harm's way.

Finally, the youth of today are hyper and reckless. They do not know their own limitations and they often try things that are beyond their ability. A wise parent will show their child the right path. We must lead our children in the right direction and show them the pitfalls they will face. Speed kills whether you are crossing a street or driving a car. It is only natural for a child who is driving to give in to the temptation to test the limit. This is when they need the words of the Bible ringing in their ears: "My son, attend unto my wisdom, and bow thine ear to my understanding: that thou mayest regard discretion..." (Prov. 5:1-2).

Children are not hungering for food. They are hungering for attention, understanding, and instruction, and to know God. They want someone to show concern for them and to teach them a better way. It is a shame that so many children do not have two functioning parents in the home. This is where the Church must step in and fill the void. The Church must provide the role models with dedicated men and women who are willing to give of their time and talent to help a lost child find a way out of the stream of tears and back into the palace of God. The least we can do is try to show them the way to salvation.

There is a song called "The Tradewinds of Our Time" (source unknown), which goes like this:

> Here I stand again, looking around me while all around me what do I see. Unhappy faces behind painted smiles, heartaches and loneliness dressed up in modern style, unhappy people living in sin and shame, reflection of myself, life is no easy game. We're caught up in the tradewinds of our time.
>
> Here I stand again, looking around me while all around me what do I see. Young girls who will soon become streetwalkers in the night, young boys, a restless breed, looking for a fight. Children both rich and poor, they're searching for

the truth, but if they can't find it, God help our tomorrow's youth. We're caught up in the tradewinds of our time.

Tradewinds are blowing, blowing around me while all around me what do I see. Hatred and jealousy, brotherhood is dying, love is the answer, but nobody is buying, good people turning bad, and for all but a few, the winds are blowing and the choice is up to you. We're caught up in the tradewinds of our time.

We have to do something. It is not enough to say, "I'm sanctified and Spirit-filled." It is not enough to say "I know the Man." Now is the time to cry out in the night, for recess is over. Recess is over when every time we turn around, we stop asking God to bless only us and ask Him to save someone else. If we can begin to reach out to someone who is hurting with a word or a song, or if we can show some father he's traveling the wrong path, we will begin to make a difference.

Chapter 9

Household Salvation

In the book of Nehemiah, we find these words:

And I looked, and rose up, and said unto the nobles, and to the rulers, and to the rest of the people, Be not ye afraid of them: remember the Lord, which is great and terrible, and fight for your brethren, your sons, and your daughters, your wives, and your houses.

Nehemiah 4:14

The time has come when we need to take back our family from the devil, even it if means all-out war. The family is struggling; it is fighting for its life. The devil is on the attack in our homes, our schools, and in the Church. As long as you sit back and let him have his way, the devil will keep up the battle. The last stronghold is at the door to the home. It is like chasing a raccoon. You can run him here and there, chase him up a tree, and smoke him out of a hole, but when he gets home, he stands up on his hind feet and squares off for a fight. Something in him is saying, "I can't go any further. You have run me up a stump, around the bush, around the silo, out of a hole, and up a tree. But now that I am home, I have no place else to go, so watch out because I am not giving up without a fight."

If there ever was a time for men and women to fight for their family, that time is now. The battle is raging on two fronts. One is natural and one is spiritual. All through the Bible the Lord speaks of salvation or deliverance for the household. Many of us who are saved don't care if anyone else in the house gets saved, but God cares. If you ask God, He will show you how much He loves every member of your family. Your family probably thinks God will judge them and cause their sins to be known by all. We need to make sure our families know that God wants to forgive their sins and remember them no more. We need to show them that God is loving, kind, compassionate, longsuffering, and joyful.

The Key Is Jesus

Many of us are so concerned with decorating our homes so everything matches, that we don't even take time to enjoy family life. One of the reasons the family is in trouble is people are caught in the web of living too "high on the hog." The family is breaking under the strain of bills, foreclosures, lawsuits, bankruptcies, evictions, and layoffs. If there ever was a time for men to be men and fathers to be fathers, that time is right now. If there ever was a time for men to stand up and be strong as the man of the house, the time is now.

We are living in a world that doesn't care if you know Jesus or not. Society is not on God's side. These are the days of soft messages that tell you to do the best you can, for after all, God knows your heart. We don't need an easy gospel—we need a strong gospel. We need to speak boldly about the things of God and show people how to get out of the rat race of life and in the race for the Kingdom of God.

It is time for us to wake up as parents and wake up as families. We are living in a difficult time and we face serious challenges. Exodus 12:13 shows us that the blood of the Lamb will save the household, but it also says there is a plague out there. The blood is only for those who are in the household, not for those who choose to live in the world. Parents need to form a meaningful relationship with their children. They need to be open to talk to them, to guide them down the right path, to make sure they don't go out the door and get caught up in the world's plagues. You must be strong in your prayer life and cover them with the blood while they play, cover them with the blood while they are at work, and cover them with the blood while they are at school. With children, you have to start early. They learn lasting values while they are very young, even from birth to six years of age. Don't assume you can keep your guard down when they are small. This is the age you really need to instill your values in them and keep your guard up. They will be faced with a number of voices as they grow up and they need to be able to discern your voice from all those that are trying to lead them astray.

Choose Whom You Will Serve

> And if it seem evil unto you to serve the Lord, choose you this day whom ye will serve; whether the gods which your fathers served that were on the other side of the flood, or the gods of the Amorites, in whose land ye dwell: but as for me and my house, we will serve the Lord.
>
> Joshua 24:15

After the people of Israel had crossed over the Jordan and were residing in the Promised Land, many of them began to practice the customs of the pagan nations they conquered. Even though God had given them a land they had not labored for, cities they had not built, and fruit they did not plant, the people had turned to other gods. This is not unlike the world today. God has acted mightily on behalf of His people, but we are giving in to other gods—alcohol, drugs, sex, greed, and abuse. We need to hear again the words of Joshua and decide whom we will serve—God or the world.

There is a call going out from the world today, and it is not the call of God. It is a voice much like the legendary Pied Piper of Germany, who played a tune on his flute and put the children into a trance. There is a voice calling to our children that is leading them down a path to destruction. They are selling their place in God's eternal Kingdom for a life filled with temporary pleasures. We need to teach them to see life as Paul saw

Household Salvation

it. "While we look not at the things which are seen, but at the things which are not seen: for the things which are seen are temporal; but the things which are not seen are eternal" (2 Cor. 4:18).

The devil is blowing a tune today and it is driving our children crazy. He has written his own brand of music—rock, punk rock, hard rock, heavy metal, and rap—and he is dancing for joy as he leads the throng who follow behind him. Don't tell me it isn't time to pray and apply the blood. Don't tell me it isn't time to seek the Lord. Don't tell me it isn't time for you to get a greater hold on your children. Love them, but be firm in your resolve to keep them on the path called *straight*. Pay no attention to their tantrums. Let them stand on their head and cry out for leniency. If you will remain in your resolve, they will soon see that you mean business and they will stop their antics.

When you tell them "no," you must mean exactly that and not maybe. When mama says, "no," daddy needs to back her up and vice versa. That means you must be one flesh and speak with one voice. This is particularly hard when the children are part of a broken home. They bounce first from one parent, and then to the other. The parents are so busy competing to see which one can get the children to love them the most, they fail to see that their selfish behavior is causing damage. Instead, they should get together and agree on the limits for the children, then hold fast to their decision. Children have become experts at playing one parent against the other. Left to their own devices, they will choose the easy path every time instead of choosing the right path.

Paul, Silas, and the Jailor's Household

> And at midnight Paul and Silas prayed, and sang praises unto God: and the prisoners heard them. And suddenly there was a great earthquake, so that the foundations of the prison were shaken: and immediately all the doors were opened, and every one's bands were loosed. And the keeper of the prison awaking out of his sleep, and seeing the prison doors open, he drew out his sword, and would have killed himself, supposing that the prisoners had been fled. But Paul cried with a loud voice, saying, Do thyself no harm: for we are all here. Then he called for a light, and sprang in, and came trembling, and fell down before Paul and Silas, and brought them out, and said, Sirs, what must I do to be saved? And they said, Believe on the Lord Jesus Christ, and thou shalt be saved, and thy house. And they spake unto him the word of the Lord, and to all that were in his house. And he took them the same hour of the night, and washed their stripes; and was baptized, he and all his, straightway.
>
> **Acts 16:25-33**

The jailor faced certain death if his prisoners were not in their cells. At the moment he faced his worst fear, he discovered the prisoners were not gone, even though the door was open and they could have fled. It was indeed a miracle when God opened the doors, but to the jailor the greater miracle was to find the prisoners had not left their cells. He knew he was in the presence of men of God, and he wanted to join them in His salvation. Like the jailor, God wants you saved and He wants your whole household saved. Paul told the jailor, "I'll tell you what to do. Believe on the Lord Jesus Christ and you shall be saved—and your house. Not only will you be saved, but if you can get your household to believe, and follow the pattern you follow, and walk worthy in the vocation wherewith you were called, your whole family can be saved too."

Some folks say, "I'm just satisfied as long as I get saved." Paul said that such a person will get into Heaven, but the fires of hell will be licking at this feet (see 1 Cor. 3:15). Some of us are so selfish that we fail to remember our responsibility as soldiers in the Body of Christ. We are selfish with our testimony, with our tithe, and with our time. We don't even want people to know what church we attend for fear they will want to go with us. When you go to work, you try to act like one of the boys rather than as an ambassador for Christ.

God has a way of dealing with a selfish attitude and with those who fail to acknowledge Him. He says, "If you deny Me before your fellow man, then I will deny you before My Father who is in Heaven" (see Mt. 10:33). It would be awful to remain smug in your own salvation only to find that, once you get to Heaven, Jesus acts as if He doesn't even know who you are. Don't be selfish with your faith. Put it out there where it will do some good for those whom you come in contact with, especially your own family.

Salvation is for the household and not just for individuals. God can make the vilest of sinners clean. I don't care how rusty and tough, and husky and musky you think you are, God has a way of making the strong seem weak and the weak seem strong. No one is too big for God to handle. The man who resists God the most, will end up falling in love with Jesus. He will make the best deacon, the best preacher, the best church member, or the best usher in the church. Once God gets into his life and Jesus becomes his Lord, he will be a new creation. Everything that he was will be put away in the past and he will start brand new in Christ Jesus. Jesus will set you free from drugs, from prostitution—from all the devil-driven sins of life.

When Paul was put in prison, he was first beaten badly. The same jailor who fell at Paul's feet is the one who beat him until he was bloody. Paul and Silas dealt with their pain and suffering with prayer and by singing praises unto God. There is strength in prayer and there is victory in praising God in a time of trouble. They were, as the Bible says, two who were in agreement concerning this thing that had them bound, and they believed God for their release (see Mt. 18:19).

Faced with a miracle of God and the love of Christ in Paul, the man asked the right question: "What must I do?" This same question is being asked of the Church by the world today. You will notice, Paul didn't tell the jailor to join a church or wait for the next altar call. You have to do more than give the preacher your hand and jump from your knees to the choir. You don't have to be saved to sing in a choir, but to enter the Kingdom of God, you must be born again.

Paul says you begin by believing on the Lord Jesus Christ. Believing on the Lord Jesus Christ means to trust, cling to, rely on, adhere to, hold fast to, support, agree, stick to, have strong emotional attachments to, and stop relying on yourself and entrust yourself to His keeping. When the jailor agreed to do all that Paul asked of him, Paul followed the man home. The jailor dressed Paul and Silas' wounds and the man's whole household was baptized in water and saved that night.

Holding Fast to Your Position in Christ

It is time we examine our household and see if salvation has come to all. The devil has staged a grand invasion on the home and some have slipped by the salvation process. How do I know this is true? When I see bickering, arguing, confusion, "fussing," and fighting, I know something is wrong in this house. God is not the author of confusion and if there is confusion, somebody is not saved. When everyone in the house is saved, there is peace. A house divided against itself cannot stand. When first one person and then another are at each other's throats, there is no need for them to profess to be saved. When people are genuinely saved and love God, they won't be at one another's throat. He has promised us peace within our walls and prosperity within our palaces.

If you are the only one in your house who is saved, you should be thankful that God has chosen you to be the first. He had to start somewhere and He started with you. If you are the first and only one the Lord saved, you need to rejoice and look at your family as an opportunity for God's greater glory. Because of you, He has a foothold in your house. If you will work with Him through prayer and begin to claim the rest of your house for God, He will move on each and every one of them. To illustrate, picture a huge rock and you standing by with a 20-pound sledgehammer. Every prayer you offer to God for your family is like a blow against the rock. Although you only see a few pieces of the rock break off the surface, inside, the rock is beginning to crack. It may not look like you are doing any good, but it's breaking.

You are bathed in the blood of Jesus and His blood is more powerful than any force of the devil. You are like the blood on the doorpost of your house. The death angel will pass over you and all who are in your house because it sees that the blood of Jesus resides inside. Because of your faith, your household is protected. Once they accept Jesus as their Lord and Savior, they will move out from under your protection and become full-fledged sons and inheritors of the Kingdom. Like Joshua, you must stand and proclaim your position in God, saying, "As for me and my house, we will serve the Lord." It is not God's will for any to perish, but for all to come to God in repentance (see 2 Pet. 3:9).

Once your family is saved, you will have to continue steadfast in the faith. You and your family will have to work to maintain faith in God by praying together. The devil will not let you go without a fight. You must be just as determined to resist his temptations and hold fast to your profession of faith.

Chapter 10

There Is Hope for Broken Homes

But know this, that if the goodman of the house had known in what watch the thief would come, he would have watched, and would not have suffered his house to be broken up.

Matthew 24:43

The phrase I want to focus on in this passage is the phrase, "his house to be broken up." The foundation of democracy lies in the home, and our homes are in danger of breaking up. In fact, many have already deteriorated so much that they are almost beyond saving. The three most important institutions in our world today is the home, the church, and the school. In order of importance, the home comes first before the church or school. After all, it was only after the home failed in the Garden of Eden that the altar was established as a way to communicate with God.

In broken homes all over the world, people have become disenchanted with marriage and family. The reason they are so down on marriage is they lack the knowledge they need to make marriage what God intended it to be. The fact that marriage is finding less and less favor among men and women does not mean it is not the best form of life for a man and a woman. Marriage is an honorable estate in God's eyes. Those who reject His plan and substitute their own will be subject to His judgment.

The devil has succeeded in removing prayer and the Bible from the schools in this country. Now he is intent on attacking the home and breaking it up before he starts his final assault on the Church. He is determined to wear out the saints of God by changing laws and perverting the times. The devil is promoting a lie and men and women everywhere are buying into it. He is sowing such dissatisfaction that wives and husbands are waking up and saying, "I don't want to be married anymore." Their hearts have been seared and their spirits are broken away from God. They are seeking fulfillment by following a false dream as they wander through life trying to find happiness.

Today, everybody wants to be footloose and fancy free and, as a result, respect for life has been lost. Respect is lost between husband and wife and between parents and children. I have often said, "Mama has the day shift and daddy has the night shift and baby has to shift for himself." In the end, everyone has the perfect scheme for instant happiness. The only problem is they have to double deal and double cross and lie to one another to make it happen. The enemy is behind it all, for if he can shake up the homes, he can break down God's first line of defense. Once the home is destroyed, there is no place to go.

People must realize that furniture or wallpaper or new cars or fancy stoves don't make a home. Those are just the things that take up space in the house; they are not the home. A home is people who are committed to God and to each other. You can have a home anywhere—in a peasant's hut or a basement—so long as there is love. Where you find a real home, you find a place where all who live there can't wait to return. If you find that you would rather hang around a bar or a coffee shop or the bus station all night, then you don't have a home.

You can have a broken home even if you live in the same house with your wife or husband. You could even be sleeping in the same bed. If there is no love, only arguing, bickering, lies, and resentment, you have a devil sleeping between a husband and his wife. Someone has failed in his responsibility. Someone has failed to keep watch over his home. That person is not the goodman of the house Jesus was talking about in Matthew chapter 24. If fathers would stand up and be fathers, and if mothers would stand up and be mothers, and if they would accept the cost of making a good home, the home could not be broken up.

Children in a Troubled Home

Abandon your selfish ways and the time you squander on self-satisfaction and use that time to get to know your children. You must realize that every child is different. Even if they are identical twins, there are no two who are alike in character and personality. One may be stingy and the other generous; one may be loud and the other soft; one may be quick and the other slow. Some children demand your constant attention, while others can take care of themselves. The days of children being seen and not heard are long past. Today, they will be heard whether you like it or not. Either you will take time to listen or they will find someone who will. Whether they need to be taught or loved or encouraged, if you don't satisfy their need, they will find someone who will.

Communicate Values to Your Child

Children should not be so fearful of their parents that they find it difficult or impossible to express the way they feel. A child is a person too and must be considered an important part of the family. There was a time when families were held together by such things as the family farm, nearby relatives, the father's work, or just survival itself. The modern family of today must find new ways to establish a meaningful connection. Instead of parents wasting their time fulfilling selfish pleasures, they need to begin to build a set of family values and traditions—enjoyable things the family can look forward to doing together.

The good old-fashioned kitchen table was often the focal point of family conversation. Like King Arthur's Round Table, where the knights of the realm gathered for fellowship and to deal with the business of the kingdom, the family table has served an equally important purpose in the past for families. Television, video games, and other modern distractions have made the family round table a less important part of the family tradition. By restoring this tradition, you will restore conversation and communication. You will have a place where you can freely exchange concerns as well as successes. By maintaining traditions that help the family stay in touch, you build a link from the past to the future.

Strong families help adolescents feel connected by giving them people to identify with and values and traditions to uphold. There are traditions in most families that reach back several generations, such as special meals, birthdays, or other observances. There is also an opportunity for new observances like camping trips or family games on a Sunday afternoon. Families who observe traditional celebrations teach their children about their family history. They introduce them to the foods, music, stories, and rituals of their heritage and culture. Family stories can create lively and memorable images— a grandfather's boyhood tricks, your first job, or a great-grandmother's journey to a new land. These family members serve as important role models for your children.

Set Aside Time for Family Togetherness

One of the ways to bring a family closer is by planning to spend time together on a regular basis. When you do come together, support one another's happiness and welfare by listening and taking an interest. Togetherness for a family must be a top priority. These family times don't need to be formal or fancy. They don't necessarily have to be the same day or time each week, although a regular date often gives the family something to look forward to each week. What counts is that they become events everyone values because they reinforce and celebrate the uniqueness of your family. Regardless of what you do to promote your family's closeness, you must be open to change and be willing to adapt your activities as your child matures. From time to time, you may want to include others who are friends of your children. This has a positive impact on the group your child spends time with and lets them know that you care and are willing to be involved in your child's life.

Below are a few questions you may want to consider. They offer examples of things you can do to provide opportunities for your family to spend time together.

1. How often does the family eat together each week?

2. During meals, does everyone have a chance to share experiences and discuss problems?

3. Is any day of the week set aside for a special family meal?

4. Does your family regularly share leisure time together?

5. Are there household tasks that the entire family pitches in to work on?

6. Are special times scheduled for family meetings?

7. Does the family attend church together regularly?

Teaching Family Values

As your children grow and develop, they begin to define the kind of person they want to be and how they want to be viewed by others. Each and every day they form their moral and cultural identities as they face a multitude of ethical dilemmas. They are faced with difficult decisions such as, "Should I lie to protect my friend?" "Is copying someone else's homework cheating?" "Is it wrong to sneak into the movie without paying?" Hopefully, your son or daughter has a strong set of beliefs and values that he or she can depend upon when faced with such questions.

Families who consistently place their actions within a framework of stated values provide guidance for a child. This framework of values helps the child deal with such important issues as the following:

- Authority figures
- Family and friends
- Moral values and issues
- Academic performance
- Unsupervised time
- Physical health and hygiene
- Responsibilities to others
- Religious observances and cultural traditions

When positive values are presented properly, they offer a clear set of objectives and have demonstrated worth. They are both universal and traditional because they affirm that every person has fundamental dignity and they promote the well-being of the individual and their society. These values are a part of and form the basis for the family belief system. You have a choice of developing a positive belief system for your family, or a negative belief system. Positive values include respect for others, kindness, a healthy life style, responsibility for actions, honesty, courage, self-discipline, service to the family and the community, and commitment to the family. Negative values include envy, drunkenness, hatred, strife, inconsideration of others, laziness, uncleanness, and refusal to accept responsibility for actions.

The values and principles you identify and act upon become the yardstick against which your child tries to "measure up." If you do not provide your child with a meaningful image, he will get it wherever he can—on the street, in a gang, or from other adults. There is a warning too: children are looking for inconsistency between what you say and what your do. As human beings, we often fall short of the mark, which is understandable. That is why we need to repent of our wrongdoing, confess our failure, and receive forgiveness. When your child sees your failure, you must take responsibility and point out your error to the child. The mistakes of life can provide good teaching material for examples of things not to do. If we, as parents, fail to deal honestly with our children, we set the stage for distrust and rebellion.

Setting Limits

As any parent knows, young people are vulnerable to many new opportunities and pressures that can lead to trouble. Shoplifting, cheating at school, sex, and drugs are just a few examples. Parents can't assume that their child knows the right thing to do. It is important to discuss these issues often with each child and as a family. Remember, teach by telling and then practice what you teach. You will find your child testing your patience and the limits of good behavior. Have you established clear and understandable limits for your children? The value of limits becomes apparent when you see what happens without them. Limits help guide a young person's behavior so he can avoid trouble before it starts. Setting clear and reasonable limits is one of the most loving thing parents can do for their child. Children would never admit to a need for limits, but they do need them and they even expect them.

Children have a way of making a parent think they have it all together, but actually, they realize they are not invincible. They are vulnerable and they recognize the extent of their vulnerablilty. This is another reason for providing them with clear and reasonable limits—it is for their own protection. In turn, parents must be aware of and give consideration to their child's needs and viewpoint. If the parent gives a child respect, the child will respect the parent and the limits set for him. Certain basic limits, such as safety, health, or family values, should not be compromised, no matter how much whining or complaining a child does. It helps to sit down and discuss the important issues in advance and to get the child to agree to the limits you are imposing. Here are a few important areas for you to consider:

- Dating
- Curfew
- Grades
- Friends
- Family chores
- Clothes and appearance
- Music
- Movies and TV
- Family activities
- Jobs
- Alcohol and other drugs

When these things are discussed, they need to be defined with a set of rules based upon reasonable expectations. The rules must also contain the consequences for breaking the rules. As a parent, you must determine which rules are negotiable and which are not. Parents who set reasonable limits help their children grow up safely and securely. They provide standards and identify important values that children learn to expect and respect.

Jesus Also Mends Broken Homes

Broken homes are a real problem. They are hard to put back together. Fortunately, we have the One who specializes in broken things. His name is Jesus. Jesus came to solve the problems and to restore a creation that is broken by sin. Jesus solved the problem of Adam's sin by paying the price and opening the door, once again, to God's Kingdom. He solved the problem the woman had with the issue of blood by healing her body and stopping the flow (see Mt. 9:20-22). He stopped the sorrow of the widow from the city called Nain, by raising her dead son from the coffin (see Lk. 7:11-15). He can solve your problem too, whether it is a spouse, a child, or you.

You say, "My marriage was to be a holy wedlock, but it has become an unholy deadlock." Don't despair; the darkest hour is just before dawn. Jesus will pick up the pieces. You say, "But there is nothing left to pick up. My marriage is shattered, my life is shattered, I've done all within my power." If you will go to God in prayer and say, "God, all I've got to offer You is a broken life and a broken marriage; a broken home, a broken spirit, and a broken heart," He will intervene on your behalf. Maybe you face a river that seems impossible to cross or a mountain you cannot tunnel through. God specializes in the impossible and He will do what no other power can do. He'll pick up the pieces and make your life, your marriage, and your home whole once again.

Chapter 11

Final Things

Marriage, family, children—none of these are possible unless a man and a woman come together in the sight of God and agree to enter into this holy union together, set aside their individual differences, and become one. This is God's way. I don't care where you are in your marriage—on your honeymoon or celebrating your twentieth anniversary; your first marriage or your second marriage—it is not too late to try God's way. Perhaps you have never been exposed to God's will for you and your spouse before you read this book. Or you may have heard someone speak on marriage, but not in this way. You might even have tried God's way, but were never really willing to give it all over to Him. Whatever your status in marriage or whatever your doubts or suspicions may be, I want to challenge you to put God's plan into action for your life right now. I don't want you to try God's way; I want you to really do what God wants you to do 100 percent of the time, starting right now.

If you are starting out for the first time in marriage, I encourage you to read these principles over again. For the sake of your marriage, take time to discuss the things you have read, pray about them, and then implement them. Begin your marriage with your eyes wide open to God's way and to the glory that lies ahead for you and your spouse. Whether you are concerned over finances, where you will live, what job progress you want to achieve, whether to have children or not (and when)—put these three principles down at the top of your list, then watch your problems begin to fade into the distance:

- Headship
- Submission
- Our inadequacies and how we can supply each other's needs

If, on the other hand, you have been married for some time or if this is your second or third time around, these principles and the material in this book should give you food for thought. If you know of someone who would benefit from these principles, then give them a copy of this book. If you are already living your marriage as two instead of one, I want you to come out of your respective rooms, give up your little fenced-in place, and prepare to restore that which you have lost. I can hear you husbands thinking, "Yeah, I have tried that before, but she just keeps on nagging me and being suspicious of everything I do." I'm sure you wives are thinking, "That man will never change. He is so set in his ways, a stick of dynamite wouldn't move him off of dead center."

The truth is, one of you must have the faith required to get God's attention and to get the job done. One of you has to start by tearing down the wall between you and letting the light of Jesus shine into your heart, your mind, and your marriage. Husbands, begin by accepting the fact that God has given you this wife to love. Assume responsibility for her and for your marriage as He intended from the beginning. She is not perfect and she never will be perfect; but she is all you will ever need if God is in the picture. Men are often on automatic pilot when it comes to women. They react with a built-in self-defense mechanism designed to prevent anyone from getting through. This is why husbands often rebel so hard against headship. They want to be in control and to boss the wife through force, but they don't want to submit to Christ or lead the wife in love. God says, "There is only one way and it is My way. Love your wife because she is part of you. If you don't know how to love her, come to Me and I will teach you how."

While the husband is fighting back the turmoil of rebellion inside him, the wife needs to be examining her faith level. Do you have enough faith to trust God completely and submit to your husband? Are you willing to exchange your distrust and suspicion for respect, love, and enjoyment? Discover your faith level and submit to him according to that level. But don't let your faith level remain static. Work on it every day in prayer and fellowship with God. When you think your faith is in short supply, God will measure out another portion to you, so long as you rely upon Him.

If you submit to God without reservation, it makes no difference what your situation is. You may have been deeply hurt and retaliated with vengeance in return. It doesn't matter so long as you submit your faith to God and yourself to one another in love. Whatever seems impossible is possible to God. He takes the mundane and makes it glorious, the ugly and makes it beautiful, the broken and makes it whole. Jesus came to reveal God's love and purpose for our lives. He died so that we might experience salvation in our soul, healing for our body, and completeness in our relationships. Thus it is through Jesus Christ that we will become complete again as God planned from the beginning.

A CURE FOR THE BLUES
by Richard D. Henton.

This series highlights how to cope with depression and hard times. These teachings suggest that "tough times won't last, but tough people do." While the scientific leaders of our day are racing against time to find the cure for cancer, AIDS, and numerous other diseases, God through His word has outlined a cure for those who are experiencing the blues.
3 cassette series $16.00
Videocassette $20.00

**R.D. Henton Breakthrough Ministries
P.O. Box 20608
Chicago, Illinois 60620
1-800-923-7111**

I WOULDN'T GO TO HELL IF I WERE YOU
by Richard D. Henton.

This series addresses the truth as taught in the scriptures on the subject of hell. While many are arguing and disputing the fact that hell is a real place, a vivid picture is painted with telling effect that clearly shows hell isn't a figment of one's imagination, but a reality. It's God's will that none should perish, but that all come to a saving knowledge of the truth.

3 cassette series $16.00
Videocassette $20.00

R.D. Henton Breakthrough Ministries
P.O. Box 20608
Chicago, Illinois 60620
1-800-923-7111

SET THINE HOUSE IN ORDER
by Richard D. Henton.
"Set Thine House in Order" is a series that focuses on the family. "There are many problems facing the family." This series highlights premarital priorities, marital relationships, and relationships within the family.
3 cassette series $16.00
Videocassette $20.00

**R.D. Henton Breakthrough Ministries
P.O. Box 20608
Chicago, Illinois 60620
1-800-923-7111**

LET'S ENROLL IN THE SCHOOL OF PRAYER
by Richard D. Henton.

"Let's Enroll in the School of Prayer" is simply one of the most needful and powerful messages to the Body of Christ. In the spiritual scheme of things, no move of God, past or present, is without a foundation in prayer. Dr. Henton is often asked, "What is the secret or key to your success in the ministry?" His reply has always been that without prayer it could never have been accomplished. At an early age God began to deal with him in fasting and prayer and, as a result, this ministry was born out of a "prayer closet." He is from the "old school," which taught him that whatever achievement one may obtain, if it's not supported by a life of prayer, it won't endure. God is calling His people to a deeper life in prayer, and these series of messages were given to awaken the battle cry for prayer. It's praying time!
3 cassette series $16.00
Videocassette $20.00

R.D. Henton Breakthrough Ministries
P.O. Box 20608
Chicago, Illinois 60620
1-800-923-7111

CHRISTIAN WARFARE
by Richard D. Henton.
Many Christians live defeated lives because they don't know how to defend themselves against spiritual attacks. As soldiers of Christ, we must know how to use our weapons and be ready for battle. The scripture states, "For the weapons of our warfare are not carnal, but mighty through God to the pulling down of strongholds" (2 Cor. 10:4). In my book I give a detailed look at several ways for believers to discover what their spiritual weapons are and how to use them against the devil.

Christian Warfare urges all believers to recapture their commitment to warfare and calls the Church to action. It clearly focuses on the fact that believers are to be more than conquerors in Christ and encourages them to put the devil where he belongs—under their feet—and to keep him there.

Retail $9.95

R.D. Henton Breakthrough Ministries
P.O. Box 20608
Chicago, Illinois 60620
1-800-923-7111